To Michael

for
deep oceans of love
mountains of encouragement
wide meadows of sunshine optimism
and still forests of tranquility

Twelve Golden Threads

Lessons for Successful Living from Grama's Quilt

Aliske Webb

The Quilt Inn Printworks Inc

1992

The Quilt Inn Printworks Inc.
24 Farmcrest Drive
Scarborough, Ontario
M1T 1B7

Printed in the USA
First Quilt Inn Printworks Printing: April 1992
10 9 8 7 6 5

ISBN 0-9696491-0-X

Foreword

If you are lucky you have a quilt that was passed down to you, from a grandmother, or even a great-grandmother. And with it you have the family's story embroidered around it. You can wrap yourself in its comfort and its history, knowing that what was passed on to you, will be passed on again. From woman to woman.

My paternal grandmother was about as poor as everyone was in 'those days'. Her quilt is simple, imperfect, inelegant. And precious. Once I left a man because I returned home to find him asleep on our bed with his shoes on, on Grama's quilt. Petty, you say. But such irreverence for things that are important to me was an evocative symbol of a relationship already gone wrong.

Grandmother's quilt hangs in my sewing room, to inspire me. To connect me. Tradition is not only what comes to us from before, created only in the past. It is what we newly create to become the inheritance of future generations -- who will talk about us in their turn. The miracle of everyone's 'now' is that we come from an unseen past and move on into an unknown future -- a continuum is implied and implicit -- from love, into hope.

Studying our old quilts, we discover the fibers that connect us -- a fabric of connections, some random, some determined. Our fingers trace the stitches; our eyes wander and caress the faded colours, the wrinkled design, the time-worn frayed edges. And our minds linger in memory. Memories that are both our own, and given to us. Handed down to us, like the most fragile, cherished heirloom.

We have a view of our grandmother as a woman who sat peaceably by a cozy fire, through long winter months, stitching away with love in her heart and a centeredness in her soul. Her truth may be something else entirely, but it is a warm, comforting image because her quilt gives us a warm, comforted feeling. The perspective of time: what we think of as 'the good old days' were known then as 'these trying times'. It is hard to imagine future generations being nostalgic about our own turbulent 'now'.

Our romance of the past is always of a simpler place, a slower pace, an easier time, because we visit it only in our minds. Like well-washed calico, history fades reality. When we envision our pioneer grandmothers we don't actually feel their reality -- we don't experience their drafty damp rooms. Our bodies don't ache from their day long labours of washing, cleaning, cooking, gardening and child-tending that started before dawn, and went on til after dark. Our shoulders and arms and fingers aren't cramped from more hours of mending, sewing and knitting, all by dim and unreliable light. All by hand, without machinery. We don't feel their illnesses, headaches, worries, fatigue. We are distanced from their pain. Pain is always personal, and separates people. Yet we can touch their joy. Joy unites.

Often we are awed by what special force of character these women had that they could forbear a physical life that would daunt the strongest of us today. A life that would bore most of us. Yes, they lacked our choices, choices that too often have left us feeling unfulfilled. We admire their sense of place, of who they were, that what they did mattered, their connectedness to their families, their world -- their community -- to themselves.

I touch an old quilt and know it is affirming that even from exhaustion, hardship, little if any acknowledgement or reward, can come a body of work that not only serves its useful purpose but that is fresh, creative, beautiful and spiritually undaunted. Here is a celebration of Work, and ultimately, of Life.

We are daughters of that tradition. How can we do less?

Aliske Webb
April, 1992
Scarborough, Ontario

October
"A Visit to Grama"

Following a business degree at college and after several months looking for work, Jennifer, my eldest daughter, was offered a job as a trainee with a bank in their Investment Services division. So today she was bursting with energy and couldn't wait to tell Grama the terrific news. She wants to be a stockbroker and make a million dollars. This is really IT for her.

Grama, actually her paternal grandmother, is eighty-five and lives in Clareville, in a 'senior's residence' - new-phemism for Old Age Home. She's been there for twenty-two years. "Longer than a prison sentence for murder," she cheerfully reminds us. The home was the best that my late husband, Jack, and his family could afford at the time. So even though we could now move her some place much roomier and fancier, she is happy here with her friends. And won't budge. Did I mention she was stubborn? You bet. I'm sure the angels have come for her several times but she just wouldn't go.

So once a month we, also stubbornly, drive all the way to visit her. Did that 'all the way' sound like a burden? It isn't. I simply meant that it's too far to pop in for tea.

We drive to see Grama. Jennifer, Susan my youngest daughter, and I, since my son Robbie is out West this year studying oceanography. The one relieved joy I have in his absence is I no longer unexpectedly find incredibly ugly, inevitably wet, yukkie creatures in my bathtub, or worse, in jars in the refrigerator. This has been a longterm forbearance, I assure you.

One high school year on the East Coast, Robbie won an astonishing first prize for his science project wherein he set out to prove that everything from the sea, or at least our bay of it, was edible. He systematically brought home, dissected, cooked and ate what seemed to be an entire zoophyllum. Much to the disgusted squeals of the girls, who naturally couldn't resist watching. I think he chose a West Coast university simply to see if everything in our western waters tastes any different.

Jack always joked that Robbie would end up a chef in a seafood restaurant, but for the customers' sake he hoped he didn't. I tell you this aside to give you some idea what the men in our family are like. We miss them.

When we arrived at Clareville this morning, Grama was finishing another quilt, sewing on the binding around the edges. This particular quilt is a deep red and blue "Ohio Star" pattern. It takes Grama nearly a year to complete each quilt, by hand. Years ago we bought her a sewing machine but she would only use it for dressmaking and repairs. Her quilts are all handsewn, with fine neat stitches. She has had a lot of practise. Her eyes are weaker and her fingers are stiffer so instead of compromising the work, she simply slowed her pace.

2

"Oh, Grama. What a beautiful quilt!" Susan enthused as Grama smoothed it out for us to see. Susan gathered it up.

"Can I?" she asked as she wrapped the soft material around her.

"It's lovely," admired Jennifer.

"It's so soft," Susan marvelled. "Even more than usual."

"Because I made it all from old flannel pyjamas and backed it with old flannelette sheets. For extra softness. It's for Mr. Fulton upstairs. He has a skin problem, you know, and he needed it extra soft. Just like a baby blanket," Grama explained.

Grama has given many of her quilts to people in the home. There are twenty-odd bodies who sleep peacefully and dream colourfully under her quilts. Some were complete strangers to her when Grama perceived there was a need for warmth, or comfort, or cheery colour, and there she would be at the stranger's door, making a new friend. And of course, many quilts have been passed gently back to Grama when her friend died. But for her there would always be a new door to take it to, a new friend to make.

"Do you ever wonder how many quilts you've made, Grama?" I asked.

"All together, oh, I guess hundreds. Yes, probably, if you count all the quilting bees we used to have back on the farm. All the neighbouring women would work like the Dickens every winter to make new quilt tops, the prettiest tops, so we could get together every spring and start quilting. Everyone would work on one quilt and that way we would finish faster. So you could say I made hundreds of quilts, by working on other women's quilts. And they worked on mine too, of course."

3

"Must have been quite a party," said Jennifer. "All those women sewing and talking."

"We didn't have TV in those days, remember, and we were eager to visit and talk. And laugh a lot," Grama remembered.

"What did the men think of you women partying it up like that?" Susan asked.

"Well, that's why we called them 'bees' -- so we could be busy as bees and 'productive' in the final report. But if the men were around, we would be quiet as mice, so they wouldn't find out how much fun we were having," whispered Grama in a low conspiratorial voice.

"Hmmm," said Jennifer, about to make one of her twenty-one year old wisdom-of-the-ages feminist pronouncements, but she was sideswept by humour as we all looked at Grama, and picturing her and her pussycat friends pretending to be mice, we broke out laughing at the truth of men in those times, and the conspiracy of women at all times.

"Now, tell me, Jen, all about your new job," commanded Grama as she patted away her sewing things to pay full attention to the bright young woman beside her. Jennifer warbled on in detail about her news for several minutes, her eyes dancing with excitement and promise.

"And so by the time I'm thirty I'll be a millionaire and buy a ranch in Colorado," she said with final conviction.

"Whoa, girl. How did we get from I-start-on-Monday to Colorado so fast?" I asked.

"I *am* going to be successful, you'll see," she asserted again.

Grama laughed, "Oh, I'm sure you will do it, honey. If you believe it and want it enough, you can

4

do anything you set your mind to."

"See, Grama believes me!" defended Jennifer.

"Grama believes *in* you. And so do I. We know you can do whatever you want. As I've always said, if you believe you can, you can. If you believe you cannot, you cannot. Either way you will be right. Belief in yourself is where you must start. But let's not go flying off the handle. You know, like the guy who 'jumped on his horse and rode off in all directions'!"

I sighed inwardly, hearing myself in my admonishing-mother role.

"Look, we all know that having a goal, or goals, is one of the most important things in life. And the first step is to have an enthusiastic attitude of desire and belief. OK, so you 'jumped on the horse' of enthusiasm. Now you have to train it to go where you want it to go."

"Some people think it is easier to simply ride the horse in the direction it is already going," Grama put in mischievously and grinned. "But you don't necessarily get to where you want to go that way. Your Mom is right, Jen. What she means by 'train the horse' is you have to develop the appropriate success habits that will help you *be* the kind of person you want to be, and *do* the things you want to do."

"So, like you mean 'riding habits'?" Jennifer laughed.

Grama chuckled at the pun and continued, "We all have habits, dozens of them. We don't even think about them. That is why they are important to us. It means we don't have to consciously think about every little detail of our everyday life. Some of our habits are good, some are bad. Why not make your habits work *for* you whenever possible?"

5

"There are two kinds of habits," I continued. "Attitude habits are how you usually think and feel. Action habits are how you behave. They are interconnected, and like the 'action-reaction law' in physics which states that for every action there is an equal reaction, everything you do produces a result, and every result affects everything you do.

"Like feedback," Jennifer nodded.

"Right. Habits are simply the daily manifestation of your character. Who you are inside creates what you do, and what you do reinforces who you are inside. That way habits, and character, become stronger. Character creates actions and actions reinforce character," I said.

"But wait a minute, let's go back a step, Jen. I would like to know, what do you mean by 'be successful'?" Grama asked Jennifer.

"Well, I guess first of all I want an exciting job. Then I want a big house, a new car and lots of great clothes to wear! I want to go to Paris, travel! You know, everything!" Jennifer enthused.

"Why do you want these things? What do they represent to you?" Grama pursued.

"Well, a good job means enough money to do whatever I want. I guess ultimately it means freedom. A nice house would impress my friends. Nice clothes just make me feel good. Is that wrong?" Jennifer was starting to sound suspicious.

"Not at all," Grama reassured her. "So what you're saying is those things are just ways to satisfy needs or feelings you have, such as feeling good or impressing your friends. Are there other ways to feel good, except through money or material things?" Grama asked.

"Sure. OK, I know it isn't the money itself,

necessarily. It's just that people accept money as a symbol of a 'successful person'. You're not going to give me that old saw 'money can't buy happiness' or 'money is evil', are you?" she objected.

"No, my budding capitalist." I looked at Grama for help.

She just smiled sagely, shrugged her shoulders and said to me, "Some roads are longer than others."

Then she turned to Jennifer and asked, "Jen, did you do well in high school?"

"Yes, of course, Grama, you know I did," she replied.

"Were you successful?"

"Yes, but that was different."

"How?"

"Because my goal then was to get the best grades so I could get into a good college," Jennifer explained.

"Which you did. Were you successful at college?" Grama asked.

"Yes, but that was different again," she answered.

"How?"

"Because my goal then was to land a good job when I graduated college," she defended. "It's only out working that I can work toward 'real' success. School was just practice."

"Jen, honey, nothing is 'just practice'. It is all 'for real'. Life is not a dress rehearsal, remember, all of life is the real thing," Grama admonished her gently.

"In any event, you were successful, or felt successful, at different times for different reasons, relative to your goal at that time. Is is possible then that success is measured by different criteria at different times of your life? And acquiring things may be just one, of many, ways to measure success?" Grama concluded.

"OK. I get it. You want me to rethink what success means to me. But I really do want all those 'things', Grama, and I don't see why I shouldn't want them!" she started to pout.

"We aren't saying you shouldn't want, or have, all the wonderful things there are in life to enjoy," I explained. "We just want to be sure you have thought it through carefully, and know what success is to you – not what others measure it by. It's important to be aware of all your options before you exercise your choice and set goals that represent success to you. We can come back to that another time." I let it rest.

"Do you know *how* to be successful?" Grama took another tack.

"No. Not yet. But I'm going to learn," Jennifer asserted.

"Good. That's the right attitude. If you want something strongly enough, and you are willing to do 'whatever it takes' -- in this case, you are willing to learn -- then you will succeed," Grama advised her.

"That sounds OK to me," Jennifer agreed happily.

"Then maybe the first thing you might want to *learn* about is Success itself," Grama suggested slyly.

"OK, OK, I'll think about it," Jennifer shook her head laughing, "And I'll report back."

Susan had been quiet all this time. With the softest of soft quilts still wrapped around her, she had curled up on Grama's sofa, listening, but far away.

"Grama, do you think I could make a quilt? I mean, could you teach me?" she finally spoke hesitantly.

"Well, sure, Suzie-honey. I would be happy to show you how," responded Grama.

8

"What a great idea!" Jennifer jumped in. "We could *both* make quilts and work on them each month when we come to see you, Grama."

Grama and I looked at each other surprised. Although the girls have been around Grama's quilts all their lives, have watched her quilt, and still sleep under quilts Grama made when they were little, they have never shown any interest in making one themselves. Too old-fashioned. Too many other interests. Too time-consuming.

There is a Hindu expression that says "When the student is ready, the teacher will appear". In this case, the teacher had been ready for a long time and now the students decided to appear.

"Well, I'm game if you are," I shrugged to Grama and then added to the girls in my most hands-on-hips tone, "OK. But do you realize how much *work* is involved, and how much *time*?"

"Sure," they nodded tolerantly. Mothers are such a bore, but somebody's got to do it.

"Are you prepared to make a commitment to do this? Seriously prepared to follow through, no matter what?" I pushed.

They thought for a minute.

"Yes, Mom," they nodded again confidently. "We really want to do this."

"Wait a minute," Grama directed. "Let's make sure we understand what a commitment is. What is a commitment?"

"It's a promise to do something," Susan answered.

"It's also what each side undertakes in an agreement," Jennifer added.

"Yes. In this case, it's part of an agreement. Like a contract. You agree to do something and Grama

9

agrees to do something. What's going to make it stick?" I asked.

"Everybody understanding the agreement, and what is expected?" Susan volunteered.

"Good. That is exactly right. So what are the expectations?" I prompted.

"Well, I guess, we expect Grama to teach us to make a quilt, and so I guess Grama expects us to learn!" Jennifer replied.

"That might also mean she will give you some *Advice* along the way, which we know you guys are never good at taking, right?" I added. "So can we expect you to listen, respect, try to understand, and, to *follow instructions?*"

"Yes, Mom," they chorused wearily.

"By the way," I continued, "What happens if you don't live up to this commitment?"

"We would disappoint Grama," Susan said quickly.

"Yes. And who else?"

"You," Jennifer answered this time.

"And who *else*, more importantly?" I prodded. They knew this was coming. All mothers do this. I think it's something they put in the orange juice they give to new mothers in the hospital.

"We would disappoint ourselves," Jennifer answered wearily again. Susan nodded.

"Why?"

"Because in the future, no one would believe in our promises," Susan answered.

I nodded, "You would lose their trust. And so it is with any commitment you make in life. It's important that your actions never cause people to lose their trust in you. Commitment is one of the foundations of your character and it's the basis of all

10

your relationships, because it creates that trust."

"So, there is your first lesson on Success, Jennifer. And you too, Susan," Grama pointed out. "You know girls, an old lady like me has a lot of time to think about life and what seems to create success and happiness for people. In fact, I've done some of my best thinking while quilting. And quilting itself, has taught me a lot of lessons that I've been able to apply in all kinds of situations in life.

"And, I've come up with, what I call, the Twelve Golden Threads for Success that stitch together a successful life. Each thread represents an important quality of your character. How you weave those threads through your life will determine the directions you take and your ultimate personal success.

"I call them threads because, like a never-ending spool of thread, you must continue to spin them throughout your whole life. The stronger the threads, the stronger the fabric, and the stronger the fabric, the better the quilt will be. And similarly with life, the stronger your character, the more successful and happy you will be."

"I like that idea, Grama. Golden Threads for Success. The first must be Commitment, right? What are the others?" Susan asked.

"I think they will make more sense if we talk about them as we come to the appropriate point in the work we do on your quilt. You'll hear the others soon enough. For now, remember that the first Golden Thread is Commitment," Grama instructed.

"Commitment is fuelled by your desire. The more you want something, the more committed you will be to achieving it," I repeated. "Now, if you are prepared to make a Commitment, and want to start a quilt then the first thing you need to do is decide when you want to finish it," I said.

They looked at me surprised.

"We haven't even started yet, how can we know when we'll be finished!" Jennifer demanded.

"I didn't say 'know' when you'll finish, but when you 'want' to finish. Think of the quilt as a goal. You've set goals before and you remember the acronym G-O-A-L-S stands for Goal Oriented Action Leads to Success," I reminded them.

"Is Goal-setting the second Golden Thread, Grama?" Susan interrupted.

Grama nodded, "Yes. Goals are like the seams in your jacket there, they hold the whole design together. Seams give shape to the garment, and so goals give shape and direction to your life."

I continued, "Remember, the process for setting a goal is to set a S-M-A-R-T goal. Make it Specific. Measurable. Achievable. Relevant. And Time-framed. Always set a deadline. Without setting a deadline you are working toward a fuzzy 'someday', and 'somedays' never happen. By giving yourself a do-able deadline you keep yourself motivated and focused."

"How about by Christmas?" Jennifer suggested eagerly.

"No way," Susan challenged. "Don't forget we need Grama to show us how, and I have school and studying. I have to get good grades this year or I won't get into college. How about by the time I graduate college?" she counter-offered.

"Oh no, that's too long," I objected. "Again, give yourself enough time to get the work done, but not too much that you lose your enthusiasm and start to procrastinate. Challenge yourself. How about one year? By this time next year?"

12

"But we, I, couldn't do that," whined Susan. "It takes Grama a year to make a quilt, and she's an expert! I don't know anything."

"But I'm old!" Grama laughed. "There are always balances in life. You young girls can do everything a lot faster than me. It's not difficult, you'll see. Don't be afraid of the size of the finished quilt, or goal. Remember, the only way to eat an elephant is one bite at a time! We'll break the whole job down into little 'bites' that will make it all easier, and the time will go by fast. You'll see. Obstacles to finishing a project should never be used as reasons not to start! Any old fool can make a quilt if you just learn a few simple tricks. Just like life, all it takes is a few good habits. One year seems fine to me. Besides I want to make sure I'm still around to see them finished."

"Oh, Grama, you're going to live forever!" Susan asserted confidently.

"OK. One year," Jennifer agreed, satisfied.

"OK. One year," said Susan, not so convinced.

I summarized by saying, "So we have a Commitment that each of you will complete a quilt by this time next year by working on it step by step each month as we visit Grama," and we all nodded.

Grama mused, "Girls, you know, designing your quilt is an excellent metaphor for designing your life -- working on your quilt represents the work you do and the lessons you learn in life. In both cases each of you are creating something that will be a piece of your future. Setting a goal is looking ahead to the future. So an important first exercise is to make sure it literally *looks* the way you want it to. Try to see in your mind's eye exactly what you want it to look like. That's called 'visualizing' and it means to see the

13

outcome you want in your head first, as practise for the real thing. See it in as much detail as possible. Make it big and in full colour."

Grama smiled as she continued, "Also add to the picture how great you will feel when you have accomplished it. Make the picture feel real. The more joy and enthusiasm you can feel in imagining it, the easier the work will be, and the more motivated you will be to real-izing the vision."

"How do we start, Grama?" they asked.

"We start," she replied, "By going down and having some lunch. There's pumpkin pie today and I don't want to miss it. After that I'll give you some of my quilt books and magazines. You can take them home and decide what pattern you want to make, and what colours you like. You'll have lots of fun decisions to make as you both design your quilts."

"The next time you visit, we'll set up your Plan for Action to get the work done," Grama concluded as we headed off to lunch.

On the way home in the car Jennifer and Susan were looking through Grama's quilt magazines. I told them how happy I was that they decided to make quilts for themselves. It was a special shared thing to do with Grama, and that Grama was a terrific role model for them.

"Find someone who is already expert and successful at what you want to do, and learn from them, copy what they do, and take to heart the lessons they have to tell. You can't go wrong that way. Role models," I explained, "help us by giving us examples of how to achieve a goal, and also, examples of what it sometimes *costs* to do so. There is always a price to pay, either emotionally or in time or energy, or even in giving up something else that is less important to us. And by the same token, negative role models can show us what not to do or what it could cost if we *don't* realize our goals."

"That sounds like another of Grama's Golden Threads to me," Jennifer teased.

"Hmm, not quite. Role models simply ease the way. You could think of them as the basting threads that you use in sewing as a guideline for the finished stitches," drawing the analogy for her.

Jennifer continued, "So for example, I should find out who the most successful broker is, and follow what he or she does?"

"Yes. That's the idea," I confirmed.

"Mom?" Susan puzzled, "Should you go and ask people for their advice, like 'how did you become successful?'"

"That is one way, sure. Often in business or trades a more experienced lead-hand will take on a junior, or apprentice -- like Grama is doing with you -- and show them the ropes. It's called 'mentoring'. But a role model could be anyone. Even someone you don't know. They don't even have to know you are copying them," I answered.

Jennifer asked, "What's the difference between a role model and a regular heroine?"

"It's only a subtle difference," I explained. "A heroine is someone you admire, and want to *be* like; a role model is someone you want to *do* like. You may not even like them as people. For example, you may not *like* a particular athlete because she is ill-mannered and arrogant but you could follow her successful 'role' or formula in practicing every day, eating the right foods, and so on. Does that make sense?" They both nodded.

15

"Could role models be historical characters?" Susan asked. "One of my teachers said that Mother Teresa is a great teacher. I want to teach so if I studied Mother Teresa I would be a better teacher."

"That's it," I encouraged. "Once you get to know the role model, and understand them, then whenever you are in a situation you can ask yourself 'how would so-and-so handle this?' or 'what would so-and-so do now?'. Also, here is a great way to make decisions easier: create a mental 'council' of advisors, people whose opinions you respect, and ask for their guidance. Our 'heroes' in life are often a represent-ation of our Ideal Self, and this is a way to tap into that higher, better self that 'has all the right answers'."

"Could I put Grama on my 'council'?" Susan asked.

"You sure could. She is someone I would always want to have on my team!" I agreed. "One precaution I want to mention: be sure that your success model's version of success and how to achieve it is the same as yours. So again, you will want to be clear on what success means to you," I directed at Jennifer.

"Making money," she replied confidently, stubbornly.

"At any cost? Even if it means stealing or lying for example? If the role model you choose made crooked deals, would you follow their lead?" I asked.

"No of course not."

"Good. What if they worked 18-20 hours a day to 'get success'?"

"I'm prepared to work that hard if need be."

"I'm sure you are. What if that meant you never had time to date, and fall in love, and have a family? Or if you married and your work put so much stress on the relationship that you ended up divorced?

16

Would that be successful for you, even if you made lots of money?"

"No. But that wouldn't happen to me."

"Sweetie, it never does. No one ever plans to have disasters happen. But being aware of what *could* happen as a result of your choices, knowing what all the 'hidden costs' are, and planning accordingly is one way of preventing negative things from happening, or at least lessening their impact by being prepared. Along with knowing what success is and why you want it, you need to realize what it will cost you, and what it will cost if you don't achieve it. That's why we study the examples of role models – so that we can make wiser choices.

"What I'm saying, honey, is 'success' can mean different things to different people, at different times. Not everyone wants to be a millionaire. There are many ways to be successful, and many ways to achieve success. For example, Gandhi was an extremely successful person but he didn't own a thing. He had tremendous impact on his people. That was important to him. He was successful at what he tried to do for them, but even he didn't accomplish everything he would have wanted to.

"So, if success is different all the time and if it isn't measured by stuff, or what you earn, or even by what you actually accomplish, then what *is* success?" Jennifer was now perplexed, still struggling for a concrete answer.

"There is one definition of success that may make it easier for you," I explained. "Success can be viewed as simply the continued forward movement toward a goal, whatever the goal may be. In other words, it's the *process*, not the product," I told her.

"I see. And a successful person, then, is someone

17

who constantly works toward their goals. They could be successful even if they don't reach the goal," she pondered.

"Right. And when they do reach one goal, they set another. Success by this definition is not the thing itself – it is the staying on the path to the goal. If you make that your definition of success you make life a lot happier for yourself because you can be successful all the time, not just at the end. The adventure is in the travelling. To follow that analogy, if the trip to the goal lasts ten days – you only 'arrive' once, on the tenth day. But you travel for nine days to get there. I would rather be happy and feel successful for nine days than just one. And, as you pointed out, I can feel successful even if I never arrive!" I explained.

"I like that idea!" Jennifer smiled.

"It's during the travelling that all the interesting things happen and all the opportunities to learn occur. Just like your quilt projects. It will be wonderful to have them completed, but I suspect the really interesting things will be what happens along the way as you work on them," I continued. "And your enjoyment of the finished quilt will be heightened by the memories of your experience in creating it."

"So it all comes back to how important it is to have goals – Grama's second Golden Thread," Susan reflected.

"OK. I'm definitely going to think about this goal-setting and success stuff," Jennifer told us. "Will you help me?"

"Of course I will. Just as you design your quilt, goals are how you design your life. Once you know what you want, why you want it, and what the cost is, then the first exercise is to visualize it, and the second exercise is find and follow a role model," I recapped

Grama's formula.

"A role model like Grama," Susan suggested.

"Yes. Now about these quilts, girls, let's be clear. If this quilt thing is just a whim-for-today, please think carefully and decide now. Grama will understand if you want to cancel the quilt project," I prodded, but they were already flipping through the quilt magazines, oo-oo-ing and ah-ing over a colour scheme, a splashy design, and mostly criticizing each other's choices as 'stoo-oo-pid', as sisters will.

As we drove home I mused to myself about the curious and surprising turns in life one day can provide.

So we were to be plunged into a year of quilting. The Commitment was made, even though no one yet knew what "it" would look like exactly, or what actions "it" would take to achieve. We had a time-frame too. A one year Goal. They were starting to visualize the finished outcome and Grama would be their role model. As we pulled into the driveway at home I was content and peaceful. This was a good beginning, I thought. The girls were excited. I felt happy and proud of my young women. There would be lots more to learn in the coming year.

Golden Thread #1

Make a Commitment

Golden Thread #2

Set a Goal

November
"FIRST STEPS"

We were late starting out this morning. Grama had called with a request. "If Robbie's not wearing that red shirt with the little purple sailboats on it anymore, I can cut it up and use it in my new quilt. Have the girls picked out their patterns? Good. See you soon. Drive carefully. We had a little slippery snow here last night."

Grama never likes to see anything go to waste, wants to use everything up -- and has a steel-trap memory. Her old-fashioned frugality born in the necessities of her youth, is newly re-found in country-wide recycling programs born in environmental necessity. Old is new again.

So the shirt *had* to be found. I figure when you get to be eighty-five, people shouldn't disappoint you, if possible.

That particular shirt had been Jack's. When he died, Robbie wore it every day for a month. Even the boys at school, usually so boisterous and insensitive, backed off from teasing him about the garish shirt. I didn't have the heart to stop him. Truth is I wished I could have done the same thing myself, still held Jack around me. I only made Robbie wash the shirt, which he did, quietly, by himself, by hand. I never knew what it was but sensed there was a memory in it, of a

21

shared time, a father-son time, that he needed to keep alive. How instinctively we hold on to symbols. Thirteen at the time, it was hard for Robbie. Looking back now, I see I was lucky because keeping the three children going, made it easier on me. The pain faded. It receded as it stayed in the past and slowly moved further and further away. The shirt was seldom worn, then not at all, and finally it was released to the scrap material basket.

Now, happily, it was wanted again. Grama's quilts are always a wonderful montage of old and new, connections criss-crossing time. She collects, sorts, debates, chooses and brings swatches of colourful past into the present. Materially, so to speak, and metaphorically. Women connect viscerally to metaphors, not only in words, but in their lives. Our simple everyday acts take on deeply symbolic, and personal, meaning. Besides, it's fun to find the memories in Grama's quilts.

At eighty-five, naturally, Grama's "now" is more heavily weighted with the past, than with the future, except for the times like these when she is passing on her knowledge to others, our girls, who will *be* the future.

"This is what *I* want to make, Grama," Jennifer was all smiles as she opened the book to her design -- a riotous rainbow of colours. "Isn't it gorgeous? It's so bright and modern!"

"Hmmm," Grama possibly agreed, casting her experienced eye quickly over the page. "Well, it will certainly be a challenge for you."

"Pretty ambitious," I nodded, thinking, maybe too much so. Would I ever stop seeing her as the little girl constantly reaching for things beyond her grasp? The instinct is to over-protect, but didn't we always teach them to stretch themselves?

"If she doesn't go *blind* working on it," chided Susan. "Look at all the little tiny pieces! It's so busy-looking!"

"That makes it *interesting*. At least mine won't be boring!" Jennifer taunted back. "Like *yours*," she added under her breath.

"You'll never finish *yours*. You know you never finish anything you start," smirked Susan.

"No one will ever bother to *look* at yours," Jennifer retorted snootily.

This is a family that talks in italics *a lot!*

"Let's see your design, Susan," Grama interrupted.

Susan had chosen a simple old-fashioned pattern of "Churn and Dash" with "Flying Geese" around the border, done in muted calico prints.

"At least mine won't keep me awake at night! Or glow in the dark and give me nightmares!" Susan started again at Jennifer.

"And *this* has been going on for a month now," I sighed wearily to Grama.

Grama just smiled, ignored the banter and said, "Well, that's good. You both chose something different. Each choice complements your different personalities. Just as in a career, Susan, you want to be a teacher, and you, Jennifer, want to be in business. First of all it's important that your choices in life are congruent with your personality and your values. Congruency means 'to be in harmonious agreement'. When your actions are in tune with your inner self and your beliefs, you have contentment, or inner harmony, in your life. Us old folks call it 'To thine own Self, be True'."

"In psychological terms," I continued, "behaving

23

in a way that is incongruent with what you believe to be correct is one of the fastest roads to unhappiness and inner turmoil. Often people are not even consciously aware that they are causing *themselves* such grief, or, they won't admit they are. That is why you have to think about what you are doing, what results it will have and what it means to the truer inner you. You never achieve peace of mind without congruency between your actions and your beliefs -- that's why 'money can't buy happiness', Jen, if the money came from incongruent actions."

Grama nodded and smiled, "And the other side of Congruency, is acceptance of others. Jennifer, your design is bold, and ambitious, and *beautiful.* Susan, yours is gentle, and peaceful, and *beautiful.* You are both different young women. *Let* each other *be* different. Value and support the differences and be happy that you are not carbon copies of each other. Life is more interesting because people have different thoughts and ideas -- and 'designs' -- than it would be if everyone was the same. Know what is right for you, and accept what may be right for someone else and support someone else being congruent to themself."

I continued again, "And like us middle-aged folks say 'Beauty is in the eye of the beholder'. What is beautiful? Susan you say A, and Jennifer you say B. You are both right. The truth is: reality is how you choose to see life. You know, the waterglass is half-empty or half-full, depending on your perspective. It's how you see life.

"The process of growth and maturity often requires us to 'see' things differently. If I want Reality, or life, to change, then first I must change. I must be prepared to change how I view life. Failure to recognize when it's time to let go of an old idea,

24

attitude or behaviour, is fatal to success, for an individual, or a company, or even a society. In a world where change comes to us at an ever-increasing rate, the ability to shift thinking is crucial. If you make it an attitude habit to be open to change you will always be able to feel confident in your ability to cope, and that helps eliminate fear of the future and the uncertainties we all face."

Grama nodded, "If you are both right in your 'interpretation' of a beautiful quilt, and therefore neither of you is wrong, can you not then support each other's viewpoint without it threatening your own? Yes? Good, then take off the boxing gloves, come out and shake hands, we have lots of work to do. OK? OK."

"Grama is right," Susan acquiesced, "And like Mom said, your goal looks different than mine but it's the path we take to get there that matters."

"OK. And right now, we are both on the same path, with Grama as our guide. So how do we start this journey in quiltland, Grama?" Jennifer inquired.

"That is where your Plan for Action comes in," Grama continued. "We already discussed how important it is that your actions are congruent with your values. Now we need to address the Plan itself.

"Remember, the first Golden Thread is Commitment and the second is Goal-setting. Planning is the third Golden Thread for success, and just as you would not rely on simply memorizing the shape of every one of your pattern pieces to guide you, you must write the Plan down. In the same way that you make a paper dress pattern, your Plan is your 'paper pattern' for success. The emotional process of writing down the plan reinforces your commitment and keeps you focused on the steps you have to take to reach your goal. That's S-T-E-P-S, an easy to remember acronym. It stands for Simple, Time-framed, Efficient, Prioritized, and Start now.

"First, the S stands for Simple. Keep your plan as simple as possible. Boil it down till you are left with the most important action items. Break the whole large project down into smaller tasks or actions that are easier to handle.

"Then T, Time-frame each mini-task. Set an actual date for each to be complete by.

"The E stands for Efficient. That means we narrow our focus from all the possible actions to the ones that will take us from start to finish in the most direct way, in the least time.

"The P stands for Prioritized which means you order each item according to importance and urgency. We don't put the cart before the horse. In other words, do first things first," Grama paused as she cleaned her glasses.

The girls nodded as I continued, "You see, planning should be the easiest part of the process. It is just thinking it through logically from start to finish, identifying all the necessary actions. Planning should be easy. The execution of the plan should be the hard part. Too often, though, people become stuck in the planning process itself."

"I know what you mean, Mom. I have friends who are always talking about their plans to do something, but never get anything done," Jennifer agreed.

"Last year at school, there was a girl in my class," Susan recounted. "We hung out together for a while. She told me she had this terrific study-plan. I was interested so she showed me. Every week she showed me her schedule and how much time she had left to

26

finish her projects. Then I noticed she kept planning and replanning and rescheduling the same work, the same essays and studies, but nothing happened.

"As the deadlines approached, she came in every day with a new plan. If she spent all the time she wasted planning, on doing some real work, she might have achieved something. After a while I couldn't stand being around her!"

"Unfortunately, that is a typical example, Suzie, of someone being part-smart," I assured her. "Try not to let that negative example dissuade you though. The important thing is, once you have a workable plan, do the work! A plan is not the thing itself. It is not a substitute for the work. It is only there to keep you on track and focused. That's why it's called a Plan for Action, not a plan for plans! Do you know which is the most important of the S-T-E-P-S?

"What?" Susan dutifully asked.

"The last one. The final S. It stands for Start now! You have to *act* on the plan. Nothing gets done until you start. A plan without action is just an idle dream. Like your friend, Suzie, she never settled down to doing the work.

"On final point about Planning. If making and keeping Commitments builds your inner character as a person to be trusted, what quality do you think following through on a plan shows about you?" I asked.

"That you are hard-working," Jennifer tried.

"Yes, and what makes you hard-working," I prompted.

"Um, persistence?" Susan guessed.

"Sort of. What makes you persistent?"

"Discipline?"

"Right. Self-discipline. Do you think that might

27

be a quality employers out there in the working-world value in employees?" I suggested.

"Sure. You bet. Because they would know you are organized and finish your work without them having to check up all the time," Susan answered.

"So, do you think people can succeed without self-discipline?'

"No way!" they affirmed.

"And that's why Planning is a Golden Thread -- Number Three," Grama confirmed.

For the rest of the peaceful afternoon, Grama showed Jennifer and Susan how to create cardboard templates which are used to cut each individual piece of fabric for their designs. She then showed them how to calculate the total areas and to convert that to fabric yardages for purchase.

By the time we left, Jennifer and Susan had their Plan for Action for the upcoming year written out month by month. They had all their S-T-E-P-S. Their Plan was Simple, Time-framed, Efficient, Prioritized -- and they had Started now.

They knew exactly how much of each colour fabric they needed for the quilt top and backing. They had prepared a budget. We had agreed on a schedule to shop for material. They were prepared with second choices and alternative ideas in case they could not find what they wanted or could afford.

The whole project had been broken down into smaller tasks that were do-able in the month between visits to Grama. First, they would prewash and iron all the fabric and arrive next month ready to start cutting all the quilt pieces. After that would come sewing the quilt top together, adding the batting and backing materials and basting it all together. Then

would come all the hand quilting and adding the final
binding. And lastly, signing and dating the finished
quilt -- and celebrating the achievement. There would
be lots to do.

"Plan your Work, and Work your Plan," Jack
always said, and here were our girls doing just that.
He would have been proud.

Grama had spun three of her Golden Threads.
We had a Commitment, a Goal, and now a Plan for
Action. So far, things were working out just fine.

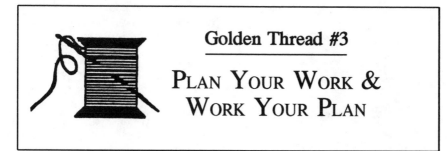

Golden Thread #3

PLAN YOUR WORK &
WORK YOUR PLAN

December
"MEASURE TWICE, CUT ONCE"

Christmas is always a wonderful and hectic time of year around our house. So much coming and going. So many ups and downs. Some friction, lots of hugs. Snapshot memories linger for a while, then float like leaves in the autumn falling to the forest floor, forming a rich soil that will nourish new growth in the spring.

I teased Robbie that all he brought me for Christmas was his laundry. The girls hung his dirty sweatsocks on the mantel for stockings. He stole their pantyhose and garlanded the tree with them. On Christmas Eve I had the last say. In each of their stockings I placed a minibox of Tide with a photocopy of the washing machine instructions. Silly family humour.

Someone says "I miss Daddy" and we are all quiet for a while.

The doorbell rings and neighbours bluster in for holiday cookies and eggnog, stamping their feet, shaking snow and filling the house with loud cheery greetings. The girls are particularly pleased with the oohs and ahs over their carefully decorated tree. Somehow I can't remember ever seeing an ugly Christmas tree.

"You know I always try to give you girls different things for Christmas," Grama explained as she handed them packages, "But this year it seems appropriate that you both have the same thing."

They quickly opened the presents.

"Grama, this is terrific! My own sewing kit!" Susan enthused. "Now we don't have to borrow Mom's stuff!"

"Borrow and lose," Jennifer corrected. "This is great! Look Mom, everything we could ever need to sew with. Thanks, Grama." She hugged Grama affectionately.

Grama had carefully assembled dressmakers' tape measures, rulers, pins and pincushions with an elastic cuff to wear around the wrist, regular needles and quilting needles, called 'betweens'. She included a rotary cutter with extra blades and a cutting board, a pair of superior quality fabric shears along with a cheap pair of scissors for cutting paper, a seam-ripper and small thread snips on a cord to wear around the neck to keep them handy. She had thought of everything.

The presents propelled Jennifer and Susan right into their quilting work. They were eager to try out their new gifts.

"Today we do some real work. You know, someone once said a quilt is a self-portrait of the person who made it. So be sure to autograph your work with excellence. That is Golden Thread Number Four: Do Quality Work. Maybe that's an old-fashioned idea. However, I will want to see you both do your best. OK?"

"It's not so old-fashioned, Grama," I replied. "These days in the businessworld people are returning to the 'old' values of quality, and service. People are tired of shoddy goods and being treated shoddily by supposed customer 'service' people. Businesses are finally waking up to customers who are saying 'I'll take my money elsewhere'. That hits them in the pocketbook."

"Too bad they are being forced into it," Grama rued. "I wish they were doing right because it just *is* right."

"Anyway, I guess we can't change that," Grama carried on, "now, let me see your fabrics," she directed. She inspected each one and finally pronounced, "You made excellent choices. These are good quality fabrics that will last. Did your Mom help you pick them out? No? Then you instinctively did the right thing.

"If you are investing the time to make this quilt, and want to do it well, then make sure the work lasts. Strive for quality. Quality work lasts. When excellence is what you put into your work, quality is the result.

"You can always just 'get by' in life by meeting minimum standards of performance, but remember that quality work always exceeds just minimum expectations.

"I've found that there are some simple Rules to follow which produce quality. Rule One is: start with the best possible materials. You've all heard 'you can't make a silk purse out of a sow's ear'. Although personally, I don't know why anyone would try! Seriously, top quality fabric, not cheap stuff that will fall apart, leads to a quality finished product.

"Makes sense," Jennifer nodded. "What is Rule Two, Grama?"

"Rule Two is: use the best tools for the job. Good tools make a job easier, more exact, more efficient. Whether it's painting a house, or painting a watercolour masterpiece, there is a right brush for the job. That's why I wanted to make sure you both have the best tools to work on your quilts."

"Guess we might have known there would be a reason!" Susan laughed and asked, "Is there a Rule Three?'

"Of course. Rule Three is: hone your skills. In other words, know what you are doing. Whether it's sewing, or handling customers, or teaching mathematics, or reading financial reports. Practice all the time to improve your skills."

"Practice makes perfect," Jennifer quoted.

"No. *Perfect* practice makes perfect," Grama gently corrected. "If you keep doing the wrong things over and over all you improve is how to do things wrong. Do the right things over and over. Make working skillfully into a success habit.

"Rule Four?" Jennifer inquired.

"Rule Four is: work carefully. Simply that. Work carefully. Think and pay attention to details. In quilting, the saying is 'Measure twice, cut once' which means you measure and then re-measure before you cut the material. Being careful prevents wasteful errors. And what would Rule Five be?" Grama asked mischievously.

"Re-read Rules One, Two, Three and Four!" we chorused.

"By Jove, I think they've got it!" Grama laughed happily, adding, "those Rules are my work-to-rule attitude habit."

Grama then showed Jennifer and Susan how to cut the fabric pieces using the rotary cutter. To explain it simply, a rotary cutter looks just like a pizza cutting wheel, only very, very sharp for cutting through layers of sometimes thick fabric. A reasonably new invention, it decreased cutting time from hours, down to minutes. For quilters, who are often cutting hundreds of pieces, it is truly 'the greatest thing since sliced pizza'.

The girls worked at opposite ends of the table as Grama talked. Jennifer, who had many more intricate pieces to cut, had decided to fold over her fabric several times so she could cut a dozen pieces at once. Grama let her continue with this method for a few minutes, then 'inspected' the quality of her work. As Grama expected, the multiple layers allowed for more 'slipping' of the fabric and many pieces turned out not to be the required exact dimensions of the templates.

"OK, let's talk here for a minute," Grama interrupted the work. "Jennifer why did you decide to fold the material the way you did?"

"To cut more pieces at once. To be more efficient," she defended.

"That is what I thought and I commend you. Willingness to work efficiently is an excellent attitude habit to have. However, we need to be clear on what efficiency is. Most people think efficiency simply means doing the work as fast as possible. We say machines are efficient and they work quickly, so we have come to make the terms synonymous."

"Unfortunately, Grama, many employers also operate that way and pressure employees to function that way," I pointed out.

"Well, that's not right!" Grama replied indignantly. "In order to do Quality Work and to be efficient as well, you have to strike a balance between accuracy and time. As you found out, Jen, the more you cut at once, the less accurate each piece became.

You will have to go back and correct those pieces. So the saved time becomes wasted time. Sometimes slower is faster in the long run."

"There are times," she continued, "when exact accuracy is not as important. That is a judgement call you have to make in each situation, taking your Objective into account. There is no absolute Efficiency: it is always relative to the objective. In this case, accuracy is important because every small error will accumulate across the quilt and you will never get it to fit together."

"So Efficiency is always the balance of accuracy against time," Jennifer repeated. She wasn't happy about it but quickly resigned herself to going back and correcting all the work she had done.

"The more you do, the less accurate the work becomes," I repeated and mused as I watched them work. "You can also take that to mean that in life the more you do -- as in 'spread yourself too thin' -- the less you are able to focus on, and excel at, any one thing. Another success choice you may have to make, Jen.

"Since there are still only twenty-four hours in a day. You can choose to do one thing extremely well, or several things reasonably well, or, you can do too many things, poorly."

"But Mom," Jennifer interrupted, "these days women are often involved in a lot of different things at the same time. Look at our friends and neighbours. Some of them are careerwoman, wife, mother, Girl Guide leader, church goer, and so on. There are so many things to do these days, that all seem to require different parts of our personality and make demands on our time. What's the answer?"

"The trick is to focus intently on one thing at a

time. Do each thing with 100% attention -- maximize your energy and time. In simple terms, when you play, Play. When you work, Work," Grama offered.

"You are right, Jen," I added. "There are a lot of demands on women. Unfortunately, the danger is, if we take on too many things, we may not succeed at any of them. It's important to know when to say 'No' and to make active decisions for ourselves rather than being forced by circumstances, or other people's agendas, into being reactive and out of control. Make sure you are making your own choices.

"A lot of women were seduced into the success-corporate ratrace simply because the door was opened to them. No one told them they could choose whether or not to enter. It became an expectation. Nowadays people are re-evaluating their choices. Society holds out the Brass Ring of 'Having It All'. For many people that is an illusion, or comes with a high-cost ticket to ride. Many people now see that that high level corporate success, in many cases is bought at the price of a human being and human connectedness. In my practice I see many lonely, stressed-out executives, who are outwardly successful, but can't figure out why their life feels like a shambles to them.

"Many women are now prepared to renounce that highest level of worldly success for a broader based, less visible and often unrewarded success in society, such as staying home to raise a family, or pursuing the career they love even if it never makes them a fortune. Having-It-All is not so great as Having-The-Best," I said.

Grama concluded with, "So be aware of the choices you are making -- how and where you expend your lifework energy, how wide or narrow your focus is. And most importantly, your choice of what will define the quality of your life and your relationships." She turned and nodded to Jennifer. "Something else to take into consideration as you define success for yourself, and set your goals in life."

I noticed that Jennifer was being a lot less defensive in these success discussions. She seemed quieter and more willing to listen. It was interesting to watch her thinking and re-examining her opinions and options.

The fabric cutting was incomplete by the end of the day so Grama sent Jennifer and Susan home with the reminder to have all their pieces cut out by next month, and she showed them how to mark the back of each piece so they would know where each one fit into the overall design.

In the car on the way home I wanted to pursue another aspect of Work with the girls. "What's the most important aspect of work itself, in the sense of your job or employment?" I asked.

"Like Grama said," Susan started, thinking a review of today's Golden Thread Number Four on Quality Work was being called for, "start with the best materials. Use the right tools. Hone your skills. Work carefully."

"That's good. That is exactly what Grama's Rules were. That is 'how' to work. I asked the wrong question. Let me try again. What is 'work' itself?" I tried again.

"In the scientific sense work is defined as the exercise of force over distance, but I don't think that is what you are looking for," Jennifer answered this time. "It's what you get paid for," she shrugged.

"I can't think of a clever way to get you to figure

this one out for yourselves, so I would like you to consider this: think of all the work you do ultimately as a *service* you perform for others.

"I know," I held up my hand in a "stop" gesture, "you will say if you are manufacturing a 'widget' that you are producing a product, not a service. Actually, the physical product, in its turn, services a need for the customer, so again, everything you do *ultimately* is providing a service. Jennifer, you 'service' your bank customers by providing them with financial 'products' which are in fact intangible services. Susan, you will be 'servicing' your customers, your students, by providing them with education."

"OK, that makes sense," Jennifer conceded, "But what's the point?"

"If you accept that idea, there is an important point to be made here which is: service has an 'exchange value' attached to it in the world. And the rule of thumb is that you will always receive 'rewards' in life in direct proportion to the 'service' you provide. Whether you realize it or not, your income is geared to the level of service you are providing for the company, or for society."

"I get it. So, you mean that in whatever job we choose, if we want a raise, for example, as a reward, we have to make sure we are serving our customers and serving them well," Susan explained to herself out loud. "More service creates more reward."

"Exactly."

"I'll bet you now want us to identify what *good* customer service is," Jennifer anticipated. "OK, let me see if we can do it as painlessly as possible."

"Is life these days, with Grama and I trying to teach you all this stuff, painful?" I was disconcerted.

"No, Mom. It's just that customer service is one

thing I think I already know about," Jennifer consoled me.

"All I know is 'the customer is always right'," Susan put in.

"There's more to it than that, Suz. At the bank they teach everyone first of all, to always be courteous to the customer, no matter how irate they might be. There is no excuse for bad manners. Then we listen to the customer in order to identify their needs. After that we respond to the customer needs -- and again, respond cheerfully. We always try to satisfy the customer's needs -- or explain why we cannot. Finally, we make sure we follow-through on any commitments we made to the customer, and follow-up afterward to confirm they are satisfied," Jennifer said.

"Good," I responded. "In other words, it sounds like you use the Platinum Rule."

"Don't you mean the Golden Rule, Mom?" Susan asked.

"No. The Golden Rule says that you do unto others as *you* want to be done unto -- unfortunately, that implies that you place *your* agenda or values or expectations on others -- and they may not be what they want. It's sort of like when Aunt Sarah gave you those cross-country skis for Christmas one year, when you really wanted downhill skis. *She* wanted you to enjoy what she enjoyed.

"Whereas, the Platinum Rule says that you do unto others as *they* want or need to be done unto. It implies empathy for someone else's differences, and understanding.

"That is why the Platinum Rule is the ultimate service motto. Listen to the customer. Care about them. Seek to satisfy their needs."

"And never put people on 'hold'," Susan

40

interjected playfully.

"So, to create a general statement, if we reflect back on what Grama said earlier about how you identify Quality Work, how would you identify Quality Service?" I asked.

"It would exceed expectations," Jennifer replied.

"Right. Does that make sense?" I asked.

"Yeah, it does," she nodded.

"Good," I praised her. "The only thing we forgot is to identify who the 'customer' is. In this broader service model, it could be the person who walks into the bank to make a transaction. More subtly though, your customer could also be your boss who has expectations of your performance on the job. Or, in a relationship, your customer is your spouse -- someone you 'serve' with understanding and love. In this model almost everyone can be your customer in some way.

"That shift from viewing your customer as a few select people, to viewing everyone as your customer creates an attitude habit that you seek to serve other people. That means living by the Platinum Rule," I summed up. "And since reward is a function of service, the more people we are serving or the more service we provide, the greater our rewards. Of course, there are many ways to serve and there are many different rewards."

"Wait a minute," Jennifer prepared to disagree. "I'm prepared to agree with the Platinum Rule about how to treat other people. But I don't like the idea of 'serving' everyone. That is what women have been forced into for centuries -- a subservient position in society. Mom, I'm surprised at you! That mentality doesn't support women!"

"Yeah, Mom," Susan was preparing to follow

suit on this one.

I could have expected this. "Wait a minute. Don't confuse service with subservience. They are two different things. To serve is not a weakness -- in fact it takes a truly strong ego to seek first to serve others, before being self-serving. Sometimes, it takes a Saint. In fact, sometimes it's what *makes* a Saint -- and that's not easy, to become one! It is very hard to unselfishly put others ahead of our own egos -- and that is why the rewards are also great."

"OK, I see what you're saying," Jennifer relented.

"The point is, you know that I agree with feminism in terms of the fairness of equal pay, and so on, and I'm not saying that injustices have not been perpetrated against women, but maybe now we have to consider another way of seeing life. I think it's time women, we, stopped seeing our social history of being in a serving capacity, as something totally negative. The skills and qualities women have been allowed to develop are the skills and qualities that everyone will need to carry us to the next century. You could say that is a positive 'revisionist' view of women's history in accord with a changed society today.

"Things *have* changed. Jen, look at all your business books. The economic model, or ideal, is rapidly moving toward a globalized service model. Information technology, for example, is a totally service-oriented marketplace.

"Service calls for the best interpersonal communication skills. Companies, and the executives and clerks in those companies, are being called on to provide this. Women have the expertise in those skills such as empathetic listening and nurturing of others -- sometimes called 'empowerment' now, or putting others ahead of one's self to find win-win solutions, genuine caring and support of the individual. Women in business used to be criticized for being too people-oriented. Now the model *is* to be people-oriented. We have the aptitude that is called for. It's time to cash in those chips.

"Don't expect many men, yet, to admit it, but their model of future economic success, is the feminine model of human dynamics. They are, knowingly or not, taking lessons from the women in their lives, and the voices of women in society. The need for hard-core feminism has passed. The enemy as 'he' was, no longer exists except perhaps as individual die-hards. Yes, there are still some dinosaurs around, and some in powerful positions, but most men have evolved into a much less threatening, and often supportive, form."

"Yeah, reptiles!" Jennifer wittily replied.

I ignored her joke to continue.

"Men know they need to learn from women. It's time to stop beating on men and take the opportunity to teach them, to help them, to create the future. Time to shift from the old self-concept of 'women as victims' to a new vision of 'women as partners'. When we genuinely believe that we are partners in life, men will accept us as such.

"This is my soapbox speech, and I think it's an important idea, so bear with me, girls. I can show you some examples of how things have changed.

"In corporations, we see fewer of the traditional army-style hierarchy structures. We now have more diffused, 'matrix' organizations. The term matrix, itself comes from Latin and means 'womb' or 'that within which, or within which and from which, something originates'. Quite the opposite of the old 'top-down' rule. We've shifted from a control model

43

of leadership to a personal responsibility model -- to the individual or workteam. It's been found to be more productive because people feel better and are more motivated when they have responsibility for, and control of, their own work. We have even seen Communism shift more toward democratization for that same reason.

"Smart companies are now nurturing and supportive of individual growth, for men and women, and are more compassionate in family matters. Management knows the company reaps a harvest of loyalty when they plant seeds of simple kindness and acknowledge-ment of the importance of the individual's contribution, and their needs. CEO's are taught to lead from their holistic 'right-brain' and to follow their intuitive gut feelings -- a supposed feminine attribute.

"Business courses now teach strategies of co-operation, or win-win, instead of competition. Look at the language of business even. The sports or warfare metaphor of business is changing to at least a more neutral one, for example, of the Arts. People who excel are called peak 'performers' or 'stars' and a manager is seen to 'orchestrate' the department. Work itself is often seen as a 'creative' endeavour.

"In entertainment, some of the largest ticket-selling events are not sports events, but stage productions like 'Les Miserables', which is a drama of human struggle and victory. Grown men go to them, and weep openly! Things have changed.

"In medicine, the male control model from the seventeenth century is finally returning to the holistic, self-healing model. The more we learn about the body and the mind, the more we learn to leave it alone, to trust its ability to self-heal. Healthy self, heal thyself.

44

We're giving birth control and the birthing process back to the people who understand it because they experience it -- women.

"In psychology, we see men struggling to re-gain their lost feelings of humanity, intimacy and connectedness. The side of themselves they subjugated for the macho model. It seems to me that in everything except economics men are far more suppressed than women. Women never had to pretend to be anything but what they are. We have always been allowed the complete fullness of our feelings, the joys and the sorrows. We've enjoyed the fullness of experience and expression and the connectedness that gives us.

"It's time to re-examine our social history and to see the positives we have gained from it, instead of dwelling on the negatives. That's why it seems crazy to me for women now to want to play the game the way men have played it. Supposedly in order to succeed. Men have moved away from that model themselves!"

"OK, Mom, take a breath, will you!" Jennifer laughed, then more soberly added, "I never thought about it that way. Maybe that makes some sense." She was prepared to consider it. "Service is where we are all heading -- men and women -- and service requires us to be in touch with people."

"That's right. I'm sorry to spend so much time on the subject, but Work, or service, takes up more of your life than any other activity. Psychologically, it is deeply linked to our concept of Self. As Freud said, the ultimate therapy is work, and love. Work is how we connect with who we are, how we express our Self. It's one of the major ways we receive affirmation and acceptance and acknowledgement from others. That's why it's crucial to do work that you feel good about."

"In other words, work that is congruent with your values, right?" Susan confirmed.

"That's right! I have one more thing before we get off the subject entirely. If Commitment builds your character of Trust, and Planning builds your character of Self-discipline, what does the quality of your Work build in you?" I asked.

"Pride?" Susan offered.

"Yes, pride is part of it," I answered.

"I know," said Jennifer, "Self-respect. No. Self-esteem."

"Right on! Doing quality work builds your inner self-esteem and having high self-esteem makes you do quality work. Don't you just love the way Grama's Golden Threads seem to be weaving into a complete fabric of life?" I smiled. "You'd think it was all part of some master plan or something!"

"Mo-ther!" they chorused, and we changed the conversation to other matters.

A master plan indeed. Would that life's patch-work quilt always fitted together so easily.

Golden Thread #4

ALWAYS DO
QUALITY WORK

January
"HOBBES, THAT DARN CAT!"

 Only in TV commercials do people sleep smiling peacefully -- with their hair in place -- and wake to the stimulating smell of fresh brewed coffee, prepared happily and lovingly by their perfect smiling offspring. I was stimulated awake this morning to the sound of Jennifer screaming. Oh, no! Was the house on fire? Not quite, not the house, just Jennifer. She was *burning*.

"You left the sewing room door open, you idiot!" Jennifer was screaming at Susan.

"I did not!" yelled the sleepy reply.

"Look at this mess! Look what you did!! That darn cat!!! I'll kill it!!!! It's all your fault!!!! Look at this mess!"

I got up. I was afraid my typewriter would run out of exclamation marks if the decibels went any higher. By this time, Susan was standing in the doorway of the sewingroom looking in at Jennifer and a chaos of fabric pieces. Literally littered everywhere. Some trailed out and down the hall, to who knows where. There was No Doubt. Hobbes, our rambunctious, nocturnal cat, given the opportunity, had 're-arranged' what had been dozens of neat piles of quilt pieces the evening before, into total cat-astrophe.

The sight of my two pyjama-clad daughters livid

47

amongst the ruins, struck me as sweet and comic and I burst out laughing, which had the opposite effect to what I would have hoped for. Instead of diffusing the situation, my hilarity only fanned the flames.

"This is all your fault!" Jennifer bellowed at Susan again. My daughter bellowing? Before I had a chance to put in a conciliatory "now, now" Susan broke into tears.

"It is *not* my fault," she sobbed running back to her room, "I hate you, you jerk!" Slam.

"It is too! You were sewing last night," Jennifer yelled at the closed door then stomped off to her room. "I hated you first!" Slam.

"Oh dear," I hiccupped at the mess, "Not one of your wiser motherings," I told myself.

Just then Hobbes, noise-piqued curiosity, swaggered up to me and sat down, totally unconcerned.

"Merow?" he asked, calmly.

"Oh, Hobbes. Now you've done it, buddy," I answered.

Done what, he looked around and blinked. Not a thing was out of place in his opinion. Except maybe this, he reached out his paw to a piece of fabric, deftly flipped it over, and looked at me.

"Exactly," I agreed and scratched his ears. "Let's have pancakes for breakfast."

Everything lay scattered as it was for two days as both girls studiously ignored their quilts on the floor. Hobbes, of course, re-arranged a few more pieces. We had reached the time when everyone knew intervention was looming, so one morning in my best Confucian manner, I taped a note on the refrigerator door that read, "Obstacles do not develop character, they only reveal it".

48

By the time I returned home from work, "someone" had picked up all the pieces and dumped them in a pile in the sewingroom. That night I noticed the light on under the door, and next day found "someone else" had sorted the pieces back into the two different-coloured quilt projects, so I did my bit by ironing all the wrinkled and rumpled and chewed pieces flat again. We were making amends slowly.

Today in the car there was still a lot of silence, and then more reheated steam recounting to Grama what had happened.

They had chosen their old pattern of competitive adversaries. Each being true to her own worst self. Jennifer had not followed instructions to mark the back of her fabric pieces so her reassembly job seemed insurmountable. Frustration for her ends in anger and a stubbornness -- she won't work on it anymore -- it can go in the garbage -- with the cat. Ever-meticulous Susan, on the other hand, had followed instructions, carefully marked each piece and managed to quickly re-organize the work. Still smarting and defensive from the blame, she wrapped herself in superior smugness. And there we all sat.

If they were expecting sympathy from Grama, they weren't going to get it.

"Since every upset is an opportunity to learn something," Grama started, "I guess there is some Truth to discover here. What would that be, girls?"

"I shouldn't have left the door open," Susan finally admitted.

"That's the Story of what happened, honey. What's the Truth behind it?" Grama coached again.

"Be more careful," volunteered Susan.

"That's good Advice, but no," Grama replied.

"Mark your pattern pieces," Jennifer sighed wearily.

"More Advice. What is the Truth?"

"That things are sent to try us?" Jennifer tried again.

"What things? Sent by whom?" Grama shrugged.

"OK, then it's not the cat's fault," Jennifer tried another track resignedly.

"Better," Grama encouraged.

"Alright, it's not Susan's fault," Jennifer again.

"That's the same as not blaming the cat," Grama pointed out.

"It's our own fault," Susan blurted out.

"That's still looking to place *blame* somewhere, isn't it?" Grama asked.

"But, it was my fault. I'm responsible!" anguished Susan.

"No! And Yes! No, you are not to blame. Yes, you are responsible. Period. You are response-able. Life is full of unforeseen events. So things happen. You are capable of responding. Animals react by instinct -- they are limited by the stimulus-response pre-programming in their brains. Humans, however, are unique in that between the stimulus and the response, or between the event and your reaction, we have a response-ability and can choose our reaction to any stimulus, or event," Grama explained.

"Responsibility," she continued, "Is your fifth Golden Thread to success in life. Your ability and willingness to take responsibility is a measure of the maturity of your character.

"Justifying yourself by blaming others, or worse, blaming yourself, is immature and defeatist. You

50

won't get far in life if you're always looking to blame your life on outside factors. Justification and blame both keep you stuck in the past. Accepting responsibility not only cuts off wallowing in destructive negative emotions, it opens the door to the future -- to learning, improving and getting on with your life.

"Being responsible means you are in charge. And when you're in charge you get to make decisions about your life instead of being blown by the winds of chance. As soon as you say 'I am responsible' you give yourself choice. Having choices gives you independence. Choice is the greatest freedom you can have. Why would you give it up?

"The more willingly you accept responsibility, the clearer your thinking will be, the better your decisions will be, and the more creative your solutions to any problem will be because you are not snarled up in those useless negative emotions of blame or justification."

Grama finished with, "The more responsibility you are willing to take, the more and greater are the opportunities you are given. Because when you take responsibility for the outcome, you are able to recognize the opportunities and are unafraid to act on them."

Grama obviously wasn't going to let them get away with feeling sorry for themselves or let Hobbes be an excuse for quitting. She dismissed the "master class on quilting" part of our visit and sent them home with a reminder of the fifth Golden Thread, of total personal Responsibility, and strong encouragement that she was confident they would 'get it all together'.

Before we left, Grama showed us the pieces for the quilt top she is working on this year -- a variation of a 'Hearts and Roses' pattern, one of my favourites. More difficult than a pieced quilt like the girls', each of Grama's blocks would be all applique work, with some embroidery as well. Slower work for old fingers, but she loved the challenge of it.

I felt a momentary pang when I noticed there among all the cut pieces were a few hearts cut from Jack's old shirt. I sighed as I let it go and thought: remember, it's all part of the ebb and flow of life. Everything is here for our use, temporarily, as we ourselves are only here temporally. I was truly pleased to see pieces of Jack's shirt, after being worn in joy, then in sorrow, passed on to be useful and comfort another life somewhere. Being around Grama's age and wisdom always makes me feel peaceful and connected. I watch her caring about people, teaching the girls, and I watch them responding to her with joyous affection.

These are special times and every month I leave reluctantly.

So Susan was ready to start sewing her quilt top together. First she would assemble each individual fourteen inch 'block', then add border sashing, and finally stitch all the blocks into one whole quilt top. For a while she was in an emotional 'clear space'. For a while.

Jennifer had a tougher time ahead. So much new information was competing with her existing ideas. She had to assess and re-evaluate where she was at and what she wanted to do. How could she be flexible and come up with a more resourceful solution without losing sight of her objective. Grama had suggested she simplify the pattern and replace some of the myriad fiddly-bits with single larger pieces. Narrowing her focus would create something uniquely her own.

Hobbes sat purring happily on my lap this evening as we mused about the day's experiences. No woman is ever a prophet in her own home, they say. Coming from me, I know the girls would have shrugged off this lesson on responsibility as simply 'mother-talk'. I remember doing the same to my mother.

How come all mothers say the same things, and all kids don't listen? I guess because all mothers sound like know-it-alls. I know mine did. It is difficult to accept advice from your parents because when you are young and inexperienced you lack the patience to listen to wisdom. And when you are the older and experienced parent you lack the patience to guide with quiet wisdom. That's why grandmothers are so important in our lives. Sometimes we listen to their ancient wisdom more closely.

So, coming from Grama, wisdom down the ages, I knew they would think seriously about it.

Seeds are planted. You never know if they will grow and bloom.

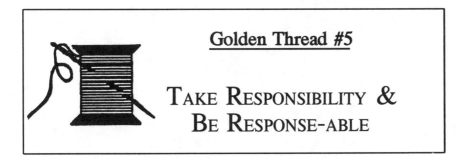

Golden Thread #5

Take Responsibility & Be Response-able

February
"STITCHIN' AN' RIPPIN'"

All was uncomfortably quiet on the home front this month. Jennifer had apparently given up on her quilt for the time being and Susan was engrossed in schoolwork, although I suspected that behind her closed door, late at night, she was quietly sewing away. Hobbes and I referred to this as 'quit quilt' and 'quilt on the q.t.'. For once I didn't interfere. Besides I knew the imminent visit to Grama deadline would bring some guilt-induced action -- quilt guilt. I'll stop that now.

In the car today on the way to Grama's Jennifer announced she had a Great Idea.
"Grama said you have to be flexible, right? And be able to respond creatively to stuff, right?" I was being sold. "Well, I have this great idea. I can take all those quilt pieces and sew them all together, crazy-quilt like, you see. That would sort of re-create one whole big piece of material, right? So then, I cut out a new jacket out of that. All I'd have to do is buy some lining and buttons and I would have a terrific -- totally unique and 'me' -- jacket. Much more practical. I'd get lots more use out of it. Great idea, right?"
"O-o-o, yuk," from Susan.
"Shhh," I to Susan.

I felt like saying, "That's the dumbest, hare-brained thing you've ever come up with," but caught my reaction.

"I'm surprised," I stalled. "Let me think." There are times when a foot simply has to come down.

"What do you think Grama will say?" I asked instead.

"Well..." she hesitated, knowing full well what Grama would think, and say.

"Exactly," I replied. "There is a big difference between correcting your course and jumping ship altogether. It's important to be adaptable and able to 'fine tune' according to changing circumstances. As long as you keep heading toward the same goal. Quitting as soon as difficulties arise, gets you nowhere

"It seems you are letting this first setback stop you and you need to regain your perspective on this disaster. You know, in the future when you can proudly look at your finished quilt, you will realize that this cat-astrophe has passed into history and you will view it as only a minor inconvenience along the way.

"Remember when you broke your leg? At first, it was painful and a big upset. After a while, though, you were able to get around and do things anyway -- it was really only an inconvenience. Time allows us to change our perspective of events like that. The trick is not to wait for the future to re-write your attitude. You can decide to take an unemotional perspective now, can't you?"

"I guess so," she shrugged equably. "I was just trying to take the easy way out, right?"

"Uh-huh," I had to agree.

She was quiet for a few minutes, then, "Grama was right you know. About taking responsibility. It was pretty painful but as I thought about it this past month I realized that if I had followed instructions in the first place and marked my fabric pieces, it wouldn't have been so bad. That made me stop being mad at Susan, and Hobbes. I know I was actually mad at myself and I took it out on others who didn't deserve it. That is pretty immature."

I nodded encouragement as she continued.

"When I'm responsible, I'm in control. That made me feel a lot better," and turning to Susan said, "I'm sorry I yelled at you, Suz, and blamed you."

"That's OK, "Susan shrugged. "I'm sorry I wasn't more careful. Maybe I could help you sort out all your quilt pieces," she offered in conciliation.

Sisters. Like kittens that scrap and wrestle and bite each other's tails. Then lie down to sleep peacefully curled up around each other. All forgiven. Unlike that old story, Love means you always, are willing to, say you are sorry.

Susan continued mournfully, "Your quilt is going to be so beautiful. Much better than mine. My quilt's going to be terrible. You *have* to finish yours."

I wondered about Susan's self-deprecating remark but knowing what a fussy perfectionist she can be I asumed she was just being too self-critical as usual. Even the best weatherman misses storm clouds.

"I wish I had known about taking responsibility before," Jennifer was telling Grama. "When I look back on my life, I could have avoided a lot of hassle and energy wasting emotion, like you said. And a lot of time."

"Unfortunately," Grama commented, "We don't always learn what we need to learn in the sequence we need it. Some lessons in life are random, even

57

serendipitous. It is up to us to fit the pieces together, like a crazy-quilt. You may actually have heard this message before, you know," Grama smiled and nodded in my direction.

"Sometimes we are just not ready to hear what we are being told, or to 'see' what to everyone around us is so obvious. Sometimes people learn the lesson, or get the point, long after they need it,"

"Or never at all," Susan suggested.

"Right. But *wherever* you start from, reflecting back from the new knowledge enables us to see how we could have acted differently and prepares us to act better in the future."

"Never too late to teach an old dog a new trick," Jennifer quoted.

"And never too soon to teach us young dogs an old trick either," Susan joked.

"It is healthy, and success-making, to look back, not to dwell unhappily on the mistakes, but in order to change for the future," Grama repeated. "The most important thing to take responsibility for in your life is learning. You are totally responsible for what, and how, you learn."

For some time everyone had overlooked the fact that Susan brought with her a fat shoppingbag, obviously full of material, until Grama finally asked how everyone's quilting was going.

"Oh, Grama, it's awful," Susan wailed, and out it all tumbled. "I just can't do this. I spent hours sewing these blocks and look, the points don't meet, the seams aren't straight and it's all lumpy!" More wailing, with tears.

Grama picked up each block and looked it over carefully. That's my baby, I thought. Where frustration leads Jennifer to anger, and kicking out, frustration leads Susan to tears and end-of-the-world anguish, kicking herself. Two sides of the same coin -- blame others and self blame. Like everything they were learning, the reality of being Responsible would take a while to really sink in and become a habit.

"Everything new takes a while to learn, Susan. It doesn't happen overnight," Grama consoled. "Which of these did you do first? This one. And which was the last? This here. OK, there now. Isn't this last one a whole lot better than the first you did? Of course it is. So you can see you are learning and improving with each one, right? You can measure your progress. You can feel good about that, can't you?"

"I guess," Susan pouted, reluctant to give up feeling bad, familiar territory for her, 'the devil you know'. She stopped moping and picked up the last block. Looking at it, she admitted, "I did feel pretty good about this one. Every corner came out even, see?"

"This last one is really good, Suzie-Q," I encouraged her. "Now what would it take to make all the blocks look like this one?'

"Guess, I would have to start all over again," she sighed, "But then all this work goes down the drain," she started to whine again.

"Whoa. Then that is just what we'll do," Jennifer ordered. "We can make a start right now. We'll just sit and rip out the seams while we talk today. Come on, Sue, where's your stitch-ripper?" she cajoled.

"No learning is ever wasted, Susan. I hate to sound like a Grand Old Guru here," said Grama, "but it looks like today's lesson is going to be on 'learning to learn'. And it won't surprise you both to hear that the sixth Golden Thread is Learning."

As Grama also started to unstitch some of Susan's wayward seams, she continued, "You know, learning is a lifelong process -- you never really get out of 'school'. Or at least you shouldn't ever think you've learned it all. Think of life as a classroom, and right now you are enrolled in the basic course, which we can call 'Learning for Success 101'. The main lessons are these:

"One. Believe and know that you get better every day. Remember, you can't learn less; you can only learn more. Every day you can build on yesterday's knowledge and experience. That's one of the great things about getting older every day -- you know more than you did yesterday.

"Two. Failing is part of learning. If you never fail, you never learn. When you were little you learned to walk by falling down -- a lot. Remember that, and know the only true mistake you can make is not to learn from the failures. Always ask yourself 'what can I learn from this upset?' And if you are going to fail, fail big. Remember, the harder you fall, the higher you bounce!

"Three. Every problem or upset is an opportunity to learn. The Universe provides everything for your enjoyment -- or your education. When upsets occur, don't get stuck in the Story of what happened -- like 'the cat ate my quilt!'. Look for the Truth under it and from the truth distill out and follow your own wise Advice.

"And finally, Four. Learning takes time. As I said, it should take a whole lifetime because there is always more to learn. So be patient with yourself."

I picked up the theme to add, "Life and experience is an excellent direct way to learn. You can also do some valuable learning by reading. Learn from others, like you did with role models. Make it a success habit to read every day, not fluff, but something that will improve you, or give you ideas.

"The trick to successful reading is: read to teach. Read so that you understand concepts, and can explain them clearly to someone else. The data is not important. Anyone can fill in the statistics later. True intelligence is not the ability to memorize facts, but it is the ability to conceptualize -- to comprehend ideas and communicate them clearly. And it follows, that successful intelligence is the ability to apply concepts to everyday life. So, always read -- or learn -- in order to understand," I concluded.

Grama continued, "To come back to today's upset. Susan, sometimes you are too hard on yourself. I know you want to do things perfectly and that is a good success habit -- aspiring to perfection. That way you will produce quality work. But you have to temper it with knowing when to be patient with yourself. Allow yourself time to learn. Which means at the start you may fail to meet your own high expectations. That is where a lot of people give up. Give yourself permission to make mistakes. That way you will continue on to success.

"Remember, every time you make a mistake, you learn how *not* to do something. Every time you learn how not to do something, you are closer to succeeding. Failing leads to success, but only if you learn something from it."

"You're right, Grama. If I could do one block correctly, then I can do them all that way now. You have to keep going, right? Like you said earlier about being responsible," Susan said thoughtfully.

"Yes. Exactly. Now come give me a big hug,"

61

Grama beamed, "and let's get on with it!"

"While we're on the subject of learning, Grama," Jennifer joined in, "I guess I should now report back, as promised, on what I've learned so far about Success."

"Great. We'd love to hear," Grama encouraged her.

"I'll try to summarize what I think you and Mom have been saying, although it's confusing sometimes. On one hand you can measure success with money and things like status symbols as some sort of yardstick to tell you how well you are doing -- relative to everyone else. On another hand you can measure success with intangibles like recognition, self-esteem, and generally feeling good about your accomplishments.

"I get confused because Success seems to have a lot of Choices about it. In both quality, and quantity depending on your focus -- sort of high and narrow, or wide and diverse," she gestured with her hands. "Whatever you choose, there is a cost involved -- by choosing one thing, you may have to renounce something else. Success can be achieving a particular goal. It can also be just progressively working toward the goal. I like that idea.

"However you define or measure it, you 'get success' first through your attitudes, then through your actions. It seems that attitude comes from your beliefs and values, and is motivated by your reasons for wanting the 'goal' -- the more reasons, the more motivated you are. Actions are important in that they have to support and demonstrate your values -- that's the Congruency thing.

"It really makes sense, Grama, how your Golden Threads all work together to create success. You have to have Commitment; you have to Set Goals; you have to Plan. Of course, you have to do Quality Work. You *absolutely* have to be Responsible for your own life, and to Learn. Whatever the 'fabric' of life you choose, these Golden Threads are the 'warp and woof' fibers that are interwoven to make the fabric," she concluded.

"That's very poetic," Susan complimented her.

"Thanks. One final observation. It seems to me that the Quality of your life equals the 'success' of all your Choices."

"That is excellent," Grama applauded Jennifer's words. "Do you believe all you said?"

"Yeah," she thought carefully. "Yeah, now that I think about it. I guess I really do," Jennifer smiled at the self-revelation and Grama nodded satisfied.

"Then what is confusing?" I asked.

"OK. It's not the ideas that are confusing, but how do I apply the theory to life? How do you know what career should you set out for? I think I understand the success 'how', I'm having trouble with the 'what'. What choices do you make, when there are so many options?"

I patted her shoulder, "You are not alone, Jen, in your dilemma. There are so many career opportunities available to people these days, it's difficult to decide. And the fact is, there may be several different occupations that would satisfy your needs and values. That is the wonderful part of our complex society.

"These days the increasing trend appears to be that people will have a series of completely different careers through their lifetime. The trick to career 'happiness' is to make sure that in each job you apply the Golden Threads," I recommended.

"I know you girls hate to be told 'you're young, just wait and things will happen in their own time', but you know, more often than not, that is what happens in life," Grama commented. "Like they say, 'you can't push the river', you have to go with the flow. In other words, you may not know for a long time what your ultimate career is supposed to be, and you can't force it. So, you may have to let it evolve. Don't worry. The important thing is: as long as you are letting your values and genuine interests guide you, you will be OK," Grama advised.

"Yeah, Jen," Susan brightened as she pointedly remarked, "You, too, may have to rip out a few seams and start all over again -- stitchin' an' rippin' -- until you 'learn' exactly what success is for you. Don't be so hard on yourself," she nudged Jennifer playfully. "Be Patient, like me!"

Golden Thread #6

MAKE LIFE-LONG LEARNING A HABIT

March
"Add Zest"

Dear Diary. Peace in the valley this month.

Susan, with her meticulous eye for detail, matched up all of Jennifer's wayward quilt pieces, and together they figured out a way to simplify the complex pattern. They replaced many of the small 'busy-bits' with larger patches which resulted in a new cleaner design. Since some of the original fabric had disappeared, gone a-stray-cat you might say, and therefore the whole quilt was going to be smaller, Jennifer decided to invest in a new complementary fabric to add a wide border, making a contrasting framework and yet pulling the whole thing together. Necessity, not only the mother of necessary inventions, had produced an attractive solution.

In return, Jennifer continued to help Susan unstitch her blocks in preparation for re-sewing them together with her newly perfected skill.

Having re-committed themselves to the work, both girls settled down to finish sewing the quilt tops before our next visit to Grama. Despite it all, somehow, we were still on schedule.

"I am so proud of you," Grama beamed as Jennifer and Susan showed her their now completed quilt tops. "I knew you could do it." Inspecting their work in detail, she proudly hugged them both.

"Excellent. Quality Work, both of you! You really worked hard and despite some setbacks, you came through. You were resourceful and determined. Congratulations! You certainly learned a lot!

"I know you both had to step out of your 'comfort zones' and stretch yourselves to get this far and I know that is not always easy," Grama commented.

"But it was worth it, Grama," Susan said proudly as she folded her quilt top over the back of a chair.

"Did you realize that you were out of your comfort zone? Because that is the lesson of the advanced course 'Learning for Success 201', the sequel, that we didn't get to last month.

"It's one thing to simply learn from whatever life hands you. But to choose to put yourself into 'scary' situations, to actively seek out opportunities to learn, that is post-graduate thinking! That is being pro-active with your life.

"Whenever you set a goal," Grama continued, "You are choosing to step beyond your present limits, and it feels uncomfortable and scary. But that is the only way you find out who you are and all that you can be. Until you set the goal for yourself to make a quilt, you didn't know you were capable of it. You will never know how successful you can be unless you set your sights higher than what you think you can do right now.

"And that is what adds zest to life. When you learn not to let fear of failure stop you, you open yourself up to getting out of your 'comfort zone'. Fear and resistence to change keeps people rooted in their comfort zones. It is usually based on their fear of failure to try."

"But how do you stop fearing failure, Grama?" Susan asked.

"Well, first of all, as we said last month, you have to be aware at the outset that you may 'fail', in that not everything we do ends in the outcome we set out for. If you accept that, emotionally it takes some pressure off and helps you relax. Let's face it, we all function better when we are relaxed.

"Remember, making a mistake is not 'failing'. Allow yourself to make mistakes -- so no matter what happens your ego won't be bent out of shape about it. In your head always play to win, but be prepared in your heart to lose."

"I understand what you are saying, Grama. But when do you stop *feeling* afraid? How do you overcome the feeling of fear, or anticipating failure?" Susan persisted.

"Fearing failure usually results from the feeling that 'failure' is bad. But failure is simply a judgement we make about an event. Remember when we talked about response-ability? We choose. We choose either to say this event is a failure, or this event makes me stronger because I learned. No event, in and of itself, is a failure. There is probably no event that can befall you that has not already happened to someone else who turned it into a success. The only difference is their choice to 'see' it as such," Grama explained.

"So, it is enough to just change your, um, attitude, and that makes the fear go away?" Jennifer asked, somewhat unconvinced.

"I'd like to say so, but the truth is anytime you are out of the comfort zone of what you know, it is natural to be apprehensive of the unknown. The important thing is you can learn to control it and not let it control, or stop, you.

"Here is the how-to:

"One: realize that you are uncomfortable, and why.

"Two: make it OK -- forgive yourself -- for being uncomfortable.

"Three: decide that your apprehension won't stop you, and go ahead anyway.

"Four: believe you will succeed, and know that if you don't at least you will learn something from the event. That way you have chosen to make every situation positive.

"I hate to say it but the more often you're in these situations the more at ease you will feel. That way the 'scary' unknown becomes the 'exciting' unknown and something to look forward to because no matter what happens you can't lose. You win either way," Grama finished.

"Yeah, Sue, like when I learned to swim," Jennifer offered an example. "I was scared at first to leave the comfort of the shallow end, but I really wanted to learn so I eventually had to 'take the plunge'. As I got used to it, my fear went away."

"That's a good analogy, Jen" I commented. "When you are stuck on the edge of the pool afraid to jump in, a simple thing in order to propel yourself forward is use a little reverse thinking and ask yourself, 'if I *don't* do this, what good stuff will I lose out on?'

"You see the real side effect and most important benefit you receive from challenging yourself is you eventually overcome self-doubt and your confidence will increase dramatically. That is the best positive motivator of all."

Jennifer analyzed. "Challenging yourself builds courage, and when you are courageous and confident you will take on bigger challenges, right?"

"Right. Is that a road to *success?* You bet," I confirmed.

"Here's a thought for you. If failure isn't bad, is success always good?" Grama posed with a twinkle in her eye.

"Oh, no. I don't think I want to hear this!" Jennifer covered her ears laughing.

"I do," said Susan brightly and added her inspiration. "Success could be bad if it makes you complacent, so you never leave your comfort zone. Then you never learn anything new. So when things change through time, you don't keep up and can't cope. What was successful yesterday, may not be successful tomorrow."

"That's terrible, Suz," Jennifer declared, having listened anyway despite her protestation. "That's almost enough to make me not want to be successful in the first place. Almost, but not quite!" she laughed at herself.

"Myself," Grama continued, "when I'm feeling fearful I remind myself that being uncomfortable is what adds zest to my life -- which otherwise could be terribly boring. Like in baking, when a recipe says 'add zest' it means you grate the bitter, and normally inedible, lemon rind into the batter to add some zip to the flavour. Whenever I have a problem I like to visualize it as a big juicy lemon. I take a grater and see myself making zest out of it and I'm sprinkling the yellow zesty-bits all over. That makes the whole picture sunnier and comical and a lot less forbidding. In other words, it helps to keep your sense of humour and not take yourself too seriously.

"After all, God gave us a neck for us to stick it out!" Grama laughed at herself then with, "And gosh listen to me, would you. I sure come up with some goofy ideas!"

"You always make sense to me, Grama. You sound like that wise Yoda character from the movie Star Wars," Jennifer teased.

"That would make you our Yoda-Grama. Yoda-Grama! What a great name!" Susan laughed.

Quick as a flash, Jennifer started to sing a take-off of the refrain from the song 'Cinderella, Rockefella' that sounded so much like what Susan had just said.

"Yo' de Grama. Yo' de Grama, that rocks me. Yoda-Grama. Yoda-Grama!"

Sometimes she's so sharp it's a wonder she doesn't cut herself. However, Susan and I joined in the second verse, anyway. "Yoda-Grama, Yoda-Grama that rocks me!" Grama laughed and shook her head as we started into an impromptu hula dance along with our serenade.

From then on, it seems not a lot of 'real' work was done today. It became a day of light-heartedness and feeling good about reaching a mini-goal along the way -- the quilt tops were complete. A day of celebration. This work was more important.

Grama had taught Jennifer and Susan the first six Golden Threads of Commitment, Goal-setting, Planning, Quality Work, Responsibility and Learning. These were all important and serious lessons to learn. Life has a lot of those serious lessons to learn. Fortunately, Grama also made sure they were having fun along the way, and were already feeling a sense of accomplishment, acknowledging the achievement so far.

"*Lock* in the *good* times," Jack used to say, closing his fist in a passionate 'Yes' gesture. So often, too often, the tough times are recorded, analyzed, emphasized and agonized over -- held onto far too long. Yet we let the joyous, whimsical times slip ephemerally away, unappreciated.

Golden Thread #1

MAKE A COMMITMENT

Golden Thread #2

SET A GOAL

Golden Thread #3

PLAN YOUR WORK & WORK YOUR PLAN

Golden Thread #4

ALWAYS DO QUALITY WORK

Golden Thread #5

TAKE RESPONSIBILITY & BE RESPONSE-ABLE

Golden Thread #6

MAKE LIFE-LONG LEARNING A HABIT

April
"SISTERS"

Spring rolled around with its usual mix of late storms and early blooms.

Last month having the girls practice by putting her completed "Hearts and Roses" quilt top together with the backing fabric and batting material, Grama had shown them the next step. Jennifer and Susan therefore had been assigned the fairly easy task of preparing their own quilt tops for the final hand quilting. First, they would lightly trace, in pencil, their chosen quilting patterns onto the quilt top. These lines would act as guidelines for the final quilting stitches.

Then, they would lay the large piece of backing fabric on the floor and add a layer of soft batting material. Finally they would smooth the quilt top out flat on top. With long running stitches they basted the three layers firmly together in a large grid pattern so the layers wouldn't shift or wrinkle as they worked on them. A lot of quilters shortcut this step by simply pinning the layers together, but of course Grama insisted that they do it 'properly' the first time, to learn how, and to avoid headaches, and heartaches, later. This time they *both* cheerfully heeded the warnings of experience and accepted her instructions.

The girls didn't know as we drove to Grama's today that in the trunk of the car was a portable, collapsible quilting frame I bought for them. They had both persevered to this point and the effort was worth an appropriate reward. And another "best tool" to reinforce Grama's Golden Thread on Quality Work. Little did I realize this, too, was going to cause Jennifer and Susan further upset and an opportunity to teach themselves a valuable lesson.

On the way to Clareville, Susan asked if we could stop and pick up some flowers for Grama. She was chuckling mysteriously to herself when she climbed back into the car with her purchase and then all the way to Clareville. We were able to join in, however, when Grama unwrapped the flowers: 'zesty' yellow tulips!

But that wasn't her only surprise.

"I thought about your 'add zest' suggestion, Yoda-Grama, and decided to change my quilt. It was too, um, conservative, and safe. So what do you think?" shyly she unfolded her work. We were astonished. Susan had again carefully, and this time secretly, unstitched part of each block and replaced some of her original choice of muted beige pieces with a new sunny yellow fabric. The effect was electrifying. The quilt top now sparkled. It had come alive. What had been safe and pretty was now exciting and unique.

"This is amazing!" Jennifer congratulated Susan and we all enthused about the difference one simple colour change made. It was an excellent example of leverage -- how a small well-chosen change had a much larger, dramatic impact.

"I really like it this way better," admitted Susan.

"I wasn't sure it was going to work out but I had to take the chance. Now, this quilt will always remind me to get out of my comfort zone and add zest. Just like Yoda-Grama says!"

Like the quilt, Susan herself, seemed to shine with a new confident determination. She had given herself permission to try! In the metaphor of her quilt and the feeling it would continue to evoke in her, she had also given herself a graphic reminder to always challenge herself.

We were all so excited we had trouble settling down again but after some more minutes of exclamation and congratulation and then some general what's-new talk, Grama suggested they start to work. In order to teach Jennifer and Susan the quilting stitch, she had prepared two sample blocks from scraps, in small hand-held lap-size frames.

"The ideal stitch is small and straight and evenly spaced," instructed Grama as she demonstrated. "It's as simple as that, though by now it won't surprise you to find that sometimes you have to work very hard to make things simple. That's a paradox of the universe -- that it's easy to make things hard, and hard to make things easy!"

While they practiced I slipped out to the car to retrieve their new quilt frame and assemble it.

"OK, there she is finally," I 'dusted' my hands as I stepped back from the now assembled frame. It had only taken me twenty minutes -- fifteen minutes of struggling without reading the instructions, and five minutes after reading them. The three all-knowing women of ancient wisdom just watched me and shook their heads pityingly. Never mind them. I never follow manufacturers' instructions. Call it a foible. It was one of those infuriating, endearing quirks that

Jack always teased me about. Ever since we were first married and I tried to change the vacuum cleaner bag and ended up blowing the dirt back out, all over our new carpet.

So Jennifer comes by her rashness naturally, you say. Of course, I could easily do things 'by the book' the first time, but I choose not to. It's a way to hold Jack near me still, to still feel his tolerant affection. An invisible shirt, you see, that I can still wear.

I must be crazy to admit this.

Fortunately, I always tell the girls to 'follow the teaching, not the teacher'. After all, we are all imperfect in some way, some time, and we don't always do what we know is best. If you expect perfection from the teacher in order to validate the teaching, you are bound to be disappointed eventually. And if that leads you to discount or discredit the teaching, you lose the valuable, valid lesson, I tell them.

"How's it look?" I asked.

"Perfect," said Susan obviously humouring me.

"The only problem as I see it," I said, "is we have two quilts and only one frame."

"No problem," asserted Jennifer as if she had already anticipated this. "We'll just work out a schedule of when each of us gets to use it."

"We can alternate," confirmed Susan genially.

"OK," I shrugged to Grama. "Whatever you think best."

"Speaking of problems leads me to ask, what do you know about problem-solving in general?" Grama asked.

"A teacher of mine always tells us there *are* no problems. We should call them 'challenges'," Susan answered.

"Oh, poppycock!," Grama snorted irritably. "That idea comes from the silly notion that if you simply use positive words in your vocabulary you will find positive, creative solutions. In the air somewhere, I suppose! Trouble is, if you *say* 'challenge', but *feel* 'problem', you are only fooling yourself, and trying to fool others by your fake optimism.

"I prefer not to play that kind of word-game. A problem is a problem. Just that. A problem, like in mathematics, is simply something that demands a solution. By definition, it insists that a solution does exist.

"I believe it's more important to work on your inner belief and attitude toward problems, than to simply change a word in your vocabulary because it's popular to do so. If you believe a positive solution exists for any problem, then you will find it. But you have to have a *process* to do so. 'Challenges', Ha!" Grama was really irked on this one. No one ever said wise old ladies always have to be sweet-tempered.

"Is problem-solving a Golden Thread?" Susan ventured innocently, eager to anticipate the next lesson.

"No, little goose," Grama patted her cheek. "It's just plain old common sense.

"Look. Here's a problem for you," she continued brusquely. "Take this piece of paper, draw nine dots on it like this:

       •   •   •

       •   •   •

       •   •   •

"Now put your pencil on one of the dots, and without lifting the pencil, connect all nine dots, using only four straight lines. It can be done," she promised.

The girls did as she told, and quickly found they couldn't do it. Grama sat back and watched them struggle for several minutes until they finally gave up, and she said, "There now. The solution is this," and she quickly showed them the answer:

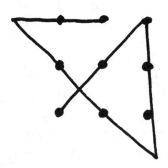

"What happened here is: you gave up. There was a solution, but you gave up before you found it. What does that tell you? I don't mean to be hard on you, but this was a simple little problem. What will happen when you face a really tough problem in life?

The girls looked chagrined. "Oops!" Jen said.

"The *problem* is, you *assumed* that you had to stay inside the square that the dots seemed to form. I didn't tell you that. The solution lies in going outside the dots. Solutions to problems often lie outside our assumptions. Assumptions can be fatal to creative solutions, and rigidly holding onto an assumption is absolutely fatal to creativity itself. So remember, examine your assumptions and change your point of view if necessary. That's the first part of the process.

"The next thing is: people waste too much time focusing on the problem, instead of on the solution. Don't re-examine the problem over and over. Instead, start by re-stating the problem in terms of an Objective -- what do you want to have happen. You should spend only 20% of your time and energy on understanding the problem and identifying the limiting step or resource that creates the problem. More importantly, focus 80% of your time and energy on the solution.

"Then, because the problem-solving part of your brain works automatically and will respond to whatever you ask it, ask the right questions. Ask effective questions. Ask 'how' questions, not 'why' questions. 'Why' keeps you stuck in what happened; ' 'Why' questions generate reasons, and excuses, and are static. 'How' gets you moving toward an outcome. The answer to 'How' questions are always actions, and solutions are always active.

"Ask questions that result in plural answers, like 'what ways, plural, can I do this?' There is usually more than one right answer to a problem. Give yourself permission to be creative and consider alternative right answers, til you decide on the one that is most practical for the situation.

"After you ask 'how' questions, your brain will 'storm' up some possibilities. Try something. If it doesn't work, stop doing it, dummy. Try something else.

"See, it's all simple common sense, isn't it?" Grama threw up her hands in resignation. "But of course, like the writer Richard Needham once observed: 'People have a lot of common sense because most people never use theirs up!'"

79

I stepped in at this point, "Often people stop their flow of creative responses because they *think* the word problem automatically implies something negative. Remember, the problem -- like an event -- is neither benign nor malevolent -- it doesn't care if you feel good or bad about a situation.

"It always amuses me to hear people rant and rail about red lights at intersections -- they sound as if the universe was personally and purposely trying to get them! It's just an event. Likewise, you choose to allow a problem to have a positive or negative impact on you."

"So be response-able and choose your response," Susan recalled. "It's amazing how that response-ability keeps 'threading' its way through everything we do in life. Problems, like failures, are a reflection of the judgements we make about them, and we can choose to see them as exciting opportunities."

"Right. That's my attitude habit -- I choose to see problems as exciting and a chance to be creative," I answered. "Personally, I always find orneriness helps," Grama now laughed at herself. "I take perverse pleasure in solving a problem, especially one that someone thought I couldn't solve."

Grama and I had agreed to let nature take its course for the next while and watch where it would lead Jennifer and Susan next.

The first week of 'scheduling' their quilt time proved a disaster. There were times when they were both free and wanted time on the quilting frame. Then there were times when each had other activities and wanted to insist on the other taking a turn. As soon as they had a schedule established, one of them needed to change because of an unexpected time conflict.

"Mom, what are we going to do?" Susan wailed as I walked in on a heated debate already under way.

"We're trying to be efficient like Grama says, so a schedule seemed the best answer but it's not working," Jennifer explained.

"Let's go back to basics," I coached. "What's your objective?"

"To finish my quilt, of course," Jennifer answered.

"And your objective?" I asked Susan.

"Me, too. To finish my quilt," she answered.

"*Both* quilts, right?" I continued.

"R-r-right," they answered carefully.

"What's your most important, or limiting, resource?"

"Time to get the work done, I guess," Jennifer suggested.

"And what are all the possible ways of working to that end? If this one isn't working..... ?" I prompted.

"Try another," Jennifer nodded wearily.

"And?" I pushed.

"Focus 80% on the solution," Susan recalled.

"Good. Both quilts. Time. Options. See you at dinner," I said as I went to the door.

"Is that all you're going to say?" they demanded, disappointed.

"For now," I promised.

There was laughter coming from the livingroom when I returned. I found Jennifer and Susan there, sitting on opposite sides of the quilting frame, both stitching away, looking like Cheshire cats, grinning from ear to ear.

"You guys look pretty pleased with yourselves," I said. "What's up?"

"We came up with the solution, of course. Just like you knew we would!" Jennifer laughed.

"We realized that we could save a lot of time if we *both* work on *both* quilts. We decided we would alternate weeks. We'll leave one quilt on the frame for a week, and whoever has time, whenever, will work on it. Sometimes it will be both of us at once. Next week we work on the other quilt," she explained.

"It should average out so we finish both almost together," Susan expanded. "This way we work as a team and we actually save time setting up and taking down a quilt every time we want to do some work."

"Sounds good to me. You came up with a real win-win solution. I'm glad. Co-operation is always a better way," I complimented them.

"Mom, we thought we were co-operating by coming up with a fair alternating schedule. What was wrong with that?" Jennifer asked.

"You *were* attempting to co-operate and that alone means you were far ahead of how most people would deal with the 'problem'. Trouble was, as I see it, each of you started from the premise that your objective was only to finish your own quilt, and you were therefore only prepared to tolerate the other person's objective en route.

"When you realized the real need was to finish both quilts then you were able to 'see' and to consider other ideas, like working on each other's quilt, knowing the other person would also work on yours, and all the work would be done," I analyzed. "You used Synergy, which meant the combined force of your actions produced a result greater than the sum of your individual forces."

"I think I understand that," said Jennifer. "But, Mom, why didn't being efficient work?"

"Being efficient," I explained, "works only in relation to yourself and the things you do. You can't *make* other people efficient. When other people are involved you have to think in terms of *effectiveness*. The final result may turn out also to be the most efficient, but not necessarily. Effectiveness is how you finally arrive at a result, but one that everyone is happy with. That may take longer, but it's worth it.

"You can take an example from business," I suggested. "For the sake of Efficiency a company may install a computer, because it works 'faster' than people. But if that results in people being put out of work, onto welfare, that isn't an effective long-term solution for society. I'm not against computers, or machinery per se, as long as we remember that people need work, for survival, and they need meaningful work to give value to their existence. Sometimes we lose sight of the fact that it is people who are important, not the systems.

"In our head-on rush for machine-like Efficiency, we have forgotten human Effectiveness. You remember, efficiency is always measured against the objective. Like the expression: when you are up to your tutu in alligators, it's hard to remember your Objective was to clear the swamp. We forgot the Objective. Efficiency is supposed to make life easier, for people, to increase the quality of life. If you created the most efficient world-encompassing system to do everything for you, and the people wither away and die spiritually because they have no meaning in their lives, then it is all for nought.

"Well, there's another soapbox speech for you. To get back to the point. I am proud of you both.

83

You really took to heart what Grama has been teaching you about the first six Golden Threads of success -- Commitment, Goal-setting, Planning, Quality Work, Responsibility and Learning.

"Up til now all those lessons have involved growth within yourself as individuals. I would call that the 'inner work'. You learn in parallel to each other, but it all took place inside each of you. As you already found out that's where success has to start, of course, in your beliefs and attitudes.

"This was the first time your goal involved interfacing with someone else, and called on your *inter*personal skills. That is the next step -- learning how to work with people. How you behave with others will always reflect the character you've been building and what you believe in.

"It's too bad Grama isn't here. If she were, she would tell you that Co-operation is the seventh Golden Thread. Co-operation is a gentle, more effective way to operate. Co-operation and synergy both mean 'to work together'. An individual can only achieve so much on their own. Greater successes are possible through team-effort.

"Do you remember the 1979 America's Cup sailboat race? Captain Dennis Conner graciously credited the win to the crew. But his wisdom chose the right crew in the first place. Because competitive sailing requires split-second co-ordinated timing of manoeuvres, he didn't choose a crew of expert sailors who by nature and training tend to act independently. Instead, he chose a team of scullers, or rowers, who were trained to row together, to act synchronously. Success went, not to the team of champions, but to the champion Team."

"What a great story. Not a team of champions,

but a champion team," Jennifer enthused and I continued, "When you come from the place inside you that believes in co-operation, you will automatically seek win-win solutions."

"Win-win is the ultimate Team sport!" Susan exclaimed.

"If we look at it, we can figure out what creates a win-win situation. What do you think?" I prompted.

"Obviously, you need a clear Objective, where both sides get what they want, or need," Jennifer answered. "We both finish our quilts."

"How do you ensure the other side gets what it wants?"

"You have to listen to them. You have to care about them, and be willing to meet their needs," Susan answered.

"Does that sound familiar at all?"

"Sounds like what we said before about Quality Customer Service," Jennifer suggested.

"Hmmm," I replied nodding, and waited.

"Yeah, hmmm," Jennifer smiled and nodded. "Service. All work is service. Service equals reward. Put your customer, everyone, on your team, and go for win-win!" Jennifer made a thumbs-up gesture.

"Terrific. OK, now how do you ensure that you also get what you want?" I continued.

"Communicate clearly and honestly. Be reasonable yet be firm," she replied.

"Good. Now what else makes win-win possible?"

"Each side has to agree on the work, on the expectations of performance and results," Susan quickly added, "And agree to work together." She pointed to the quilt, "We have to stitch as carefully on each other's quilt as we do on our own."

"Excellent."

85

"That's right," Jennifer continued. "We made a commitment, so I guess we could both trust each other, to be fair and to have the other person's interests at heart also."

"Bingo! Trust is absolutely crucial. Without trust there is no commitment, and without commitment there is no win-win!" I congratulated them.

"So, we've come full circle back to Grama's first Golden Thread: Commitment," Jennifer remarked. "She said there are twelve Golden Threads for success. What more can there be?"

"Guess, we'll have to wait and see," I smiled what I hoped was a mysterious smile. They shook their heads and returned to carefully stitching the quilt. I watched them for a few minutes, and then observed, "Grama is going to love your old-fashioned solution."

"What do you mean? I thought win-win was the newest buzzword in all the business books. What do you mean 'old-fashioned'?" Jennifer was surprised.

"Well, look at yourselves. You guys just re-invented the quilting bee!" I laughed.

They looked up from their work, at each other stunned and then burst out laughing.

"You're right, Mom, just like Grama and the ladies back on the farm years ago around the quilting frame. Here we are just sittin' and stitchin'!" Susan exclaimed.

"And," I continued, "No one ever conducted a time-and-motion study on them. No one ever taught them formal management skills. Yet throughout history women have always sought to work co-operatively, to optimize life, for everyone. I believe that is because co-operation is an expression of our higher self, our highest and best way of being human, and I think women are strongly connected to that principle."

"Pretty clever of them, right?" Jennifer commented.

"Pretty efficient," I intimated.

"Pretty effective!" they chorused.

Golden Thread #7

CO-OPERATE

May
"YES, SHE CAN"

I don't know if it was simply the energy of late Spring and the joy of warm weather coming that kept my quilting bees buzzing. Jennifer and Susan were actually enjoying their work, despite pricked fingers and sore shoulders. I often saw them sitting quilting alone with the TV or radio playing -- Jennifer's pop music and Susan's Mozart.

Just as often, though, I found the two of them at the quilting frame rooted to the commonality of the work. I also overheard bits of conversation, laughter, debates on rock versus classical music, men, and so on. Face to face, as it were, for hours at a time, they couldn't avoid talking to each other.

Strangely, they were actually communicating with each other -- listening, debating, trying to understand, laughing, enjoying and learning from the differences -- delightfully surprised by what they found out about the stranger who was their own sister. Taking a page from their problem-solving lesson, they were willing to examine their assumptions, and dropping their pre-conceptions about each other had opened their hearts to seeing the other's reality.

I was reminded of Buckminster Fuller's theory of 'precession', which roughly states that often as we proceed through life in one direction, toward an avowed goal, our real purpose may in fact lie undiscovered at right angles to that direction, with us totally unaware of it. The example of the honeybee, appropriately, comes to mind. The bee travels to the flower, or goal, 'thinking' her purpose is to make honey. However, in the 'grand scheme of things' her true purpose may actually be to cross-pollinate flowers, and the bee does not know that. Discovering our true purpose can be a lifetime challenge.

Jennifer and Susan received the unexpected gift of getting to know each other, as a right-angled by-product of their apparent objective to simply finish their quilts. Applying themselves to the work, reaped them benefits 'unforeseen in common hours' as Emerson wrote.

"Susan is going to be a great teacher," said Jennifer emphatically. "Mom, I have to tell you and Grama what happened last Saturday. Susan was babysitting Lisabeth. Grama, that's our neighbour, Mrs. Martelli's, three and a half year old daughter.

"When, I came home, I found the two of them in the livingroom at the quilt rack. Lizzie was propped up on a telephone book. 'Watcha doin'?', I asked and Susan answered, 'Lizzie's helping me quilt'. 'She can't quilt. She can't even sew,' says I. 'Yes, she can. Look,' says Susan and then explained that Lizzie wanted to help so Sue taught her to thread the needles she was using. Under a watchful eye, of course. It took her a long time to thread one but you know how focused a three year old can be. By the time Lizzie threaded one needle, Sue was ready for it. Lizzie pointed to 'her' stitches where 'her' thread was and she was a pretty proud little girl, I tell you. Isn't that neat?" Jennifer finished.

"It sure is. And it's so true," Grama replied. "There is a way for everyone to contribute. Sometimes it takes creative thinking to find a way but there is always a part for everyone to play.

"Again, if you think about your quilt, there are many different components which are all important to the whole. The quilt top is artistic and attractive and gives eye-appeal. The backing provides sturdiness. Even between the layers, the invisible batting provides a necessary quality of heat retention. The quilting stitches hold everything together and provide the definition of what a quilt is.

"And so it is with people. Even the invisible tasks or back-stage parts are necessary to the success of the whole. So there are small tasks for the little ones and bigger tasks for the big people."

"You see, making a contribution is a way of feeling that we belong. We all need to feel we are part of something -- that we matter. The person who contributes feels good, feels important and necessary. The person feels connected. Like they say, it is more blessed to give than to receive -- if you read 'blessed' as meaning it feels better.

"Making a difference is how we create a sense of Purpose in our lives."

"So, Contribution must be Golden Thread Number Eight, right?" Susan anticipated.

"That's right," Grama continued. "There are many levels at which to contribute. The more successful you are, in terms of accomplishment, money, knowledge, or whatever, the more you are able, and should, contribute. When we succeed at anything we are obliged to turn around and give back, in some way, to help someone else to succeed.

"That is the concept of 'tithing'. It doesn't just

91

mean giving money to a church or charity. It means working in a way that ensures everyone else also succeeds. Making a contribution to society through our work and making a difference in people's lives through our relationships is the way we pay back for the success and abundance we have received.

"Contribution is Service, or Work, at the highest level. Remember that we are given rewards in life in proportion to the service we give. Or, to look at it another way, 'service is the price we pay for the room we occupy in life'," she concluded.

Jen's reaction was a thoughtful but unnatural quietness. I thought I could almost hear her thinking this sounded too much like evangelical poverty. The dilemma as she perceives it -- does she pursue money and worldly 'success' or does she pursue a meaningful, and possibly unpaid, peace of mind.

Susan is lucky. She is one of those fortunate people who has always known she wants to teach. She is the deep and thought-full one who has always had a quiet sense of purpose. Although I had other concerns for Susan through her life I've never had to worry about her convictions and direction in life. Jennifer, on the other hand, is the family's squeaky hinge and therefore sometimes receives a disproportionate share of oil. She has struggled with her direction for years, changing her mind many times. Careers have been 'flavour of the month' whims.

For a child of her generation, success -- quick easy money -- is the superficial lure. Quieter moments of introspective discussion reveal the deeper value-driven foundation of her character which struggles to reconcile with her 'stuff goals'. Many gab sessions have revealed these ambiguous, apparently mutually exclusive, desires.

As I tuned back into the conversation, Grama was continuing her thoughts.

"You know the expression 'what goes around, comes around'?" The girls nodded yes. "It has a sort of 'revenge' connotation to it, doesn't it? A sort of 'you'll get yours', or literally that we will reap what we sow. I think it also has a deeper meaning. I sincerely believe that the Universe, or God if you prefer, co-operates with good endeavours. The more you give, the more you receive, and the more you have to give."

Grama left them with that thought for a minute, then continued, "Most of what we do in life, we do for ourselves. Contribution is how we strike a balance by being self-less. Everything needs a balance. Light and dark. Yin and yang. Summer and winter. For all the selfish pursuits we have, we need a self-less counterweight. That's how the universe stays in balance."

"You see, Jen, you may find that it isn't a simple 'and/or' situation after all," I suggested. "You are not necessarily condemned to choosing between a purposeful life and a comfortable life, or between meaningfulness and materialism."

"But how can the two be reconciled?" she struggled.

"Think about your quilt again," I explained. "Think, if you will, about the 'essence of quiltness'. A quilt has a purpose, right? It can serve the useful function on a bed of keeping someone warm. A quilt also has an aesthetic, eye-pleasing aspect through its external 'material' design. The two aspects are interwoven and balanced.

"If you remove purpose from the quilt, or from life, you are left with artifice and no substance. If you

93

remove the pleasurable aesthetic quality from your quilt, or life, it becomes flat, colourless, without spirit or emotive-power. Does that make sense to you?"

Jennifer nodded slowly, "I think I understand what you're saying. I have to design goals for my life that take both into consideration. Do work that has value or purpose by making a difference. Yet it should also be work that I enjoy and that uses my talents." Again she nodded thoughtfully. "I like the idea that success is the process of working toward a goal, not the goal itself -- but that it's OK to want the 'stuff', too."

I nodded.

"If I understand what you and Grama are saying, I need to structure my career goals, and in fact my life goals, around making a difference, not around making money. The rewards will come naturally from my service if I am doing what is right, according to my values, and my interests and my talents. That creates Congruency between my actions and my values which is the key to happiness and peace of mind. I can balance Purpose and Pleasure," she nodded finally with satisfaction.

"Right! That's the way to start," I encouraged her.

"Great. Now I have the 'how' all stitched up. I just have to figure out the details of 'what'," she smiled.

A few weeks later Jennifer came to me, "Mom, I'd like to know what you think about the new goals I set."

"Terrific. Tell me all about it."

"Well," she paused and took a breath. "I asked for a transfer to the Customer Services Department. I decided that within five years I want to become the Customer Services Manager. I know, you are going to ask why do I want to be the Manager and you are thinking it's for the big salary, the status and everything. That is part of it, but the other reason is so I can train people in good customer service. I can 'make a difference' that way. I really do enjoy helping people and I think I'm good at it.

"I also thought I would offer a course on basic financial planning at the local high school -- to teach and pass on all the stuff I've learned -- to make a contribution." She was embarrassed. "Does that sound too noble?"

"Sounds a lot better than making a million dollars just so you can buy a ranch in Colorado," I assured her. "I think your goal sounds fine and anything I can do to help, let me know."

"Well, I would like to hear what you think of my five year Plan. There are some courses I need to take and management skills I have to acquire. Here, I have it all written out," she pulled papers from her handbag. "I keep it with me, to remind me."

"And a Plan, too! I'm impressed!" I hugged her.

Some chicks fall from the nest, some jump. Either way, fly or die.

Golden Thread #8

CONTRIBUTE &
MAKE A DIFFERENCE

June
"Boredom Sets In"

For weeks now my bees have buzzed away on the two quilts. At first they found time every day, even if only a few minutes, and the work proceeded apace. Their initial concentration on mastering the quilting stitch quickly paid off as their stitches became smaller and straighter and evenly space. They were pleased with their new skill and the results as the subtle quilted patterns spread over the quilt. They were soon able to work faster and the sewing motion became natural and automatic.

Soon it no longer took the same concentration and, as you can imagine, their interest began to wane. The expanse of surface yet to be covered started to loom larger and burdensome. Boredom had set in. Disinterested in the tedium of the now repetitive work, they spent less time at it, and progress seemed minimal.

"So, how is the quilting going, girls?" Grama cheerfully asked this afternoon.

"Fine," and "Just great," they replied equally cheerfully.

"Uh-huh," Grama nodded suspiciously. "Any problems at all?" she asked.

"No. Everything is *fine*, right Sue? We're just working away. There is still a lot to do, of course," Jennifer 'chirped' 'pertly'. We hate those words.

"Uh-huh," Grama again, eyeing them closely, pursued, "So you're enjoying the quilting?"

"Oh, of course, Grama. Everything is *fine*," said Susan.

"Uh-huh," Grama repeated. "OK, you've done your duty of making an old lady feel better. Now tell me the truth. I always know, Susan, when you say 'fine' and your voice goes up an octave, that something is wrong. What is it?" Grama demanded.

"Well..." Susan hesitated to say, still couldn't admit it, so Jennifer jumped in, "Grama, it's just so boring! It's the same thing over and over again. It feels like this will go on forever! It feels like we're never going to finish!"

"And you, Susan?" Grama nudged her.

"I'm sorry, Grama, but it *is* pretty boring," Susan whined.

"I see. Well, it looks like we need the p-medicine for two young women with p-*moan*-ia! What dosage do you figure?" she asked, turning to me.

"Oh, they've got it *bad*. Doubles, at least," I smiled.

"What? What is p-medicine?" they exclaimed.

"Girls, at some point *every* job becomes routine," Grama explained. "Even the most glamorous occupation or exciting project has drudgery-bits. The formula for p-medicine is equal portions of your p-words: patience, perfection, persistence, perseverance and pride.

"There is no way round it. A quilt takes a lot of time, to do it well, so be Patient. The best things in life, and great works, don't happen overnight. Any

98

kind of success takes patience -- you better learn it now. If you're not good at waiting things out, start practicing. And that means staying focused while you wait.

"Remember, Perfection is your goal and it takes hard work. Sometimes you have to simply 'bear down' and get it done. That phrase comes from childbirth where you 'bear down' until you get results, or perish! Persistence connotes that *stubborn* determination and Perseverance means to continue in spite of *difficulty*. Then, last but not least, be too Proud to quit or admit defeat.

"You see, the p-medicine is a 'magic elixir' that builds your endurance. Having stamina means you survive long enough to succeed. Too often people give up just a few steps from success. If you just hang in there, your goal may be right around the corner," Grama concluded.

"I like that," Jennifer enthused. "So next time I'm suffering from p-moan-ia, I'll stand up and yell 'I'm p'd off!'," she laughed.

"Then just sit down and continue working anyway?" Susan questioned with a shrug.

I stepped in then with, "There are also some other actions you can take to feel better and help yourself cope with boredom and the 'down times'. First of all, when you are faced with something arduous that you *have to* do, *will* what you have to do. In other words, decide to consciously *choose* to do it."

"In other words," Jennifer interrupted, "What you are saying is, be response-able and *choose* to do it."

"Exactly," Grama confirmed. "Always remember you are doing something because you chose to do it. Nobody forces you, except you. You want to finish the quilt. Remember your original enthusiasm and excitement, and recall your initial visualization you created of how great you will feel when you finish the quilt."

"Another simple thing you can do," I suggested, "Is to break the long task into smaller ones. Remember Golden Thread #3: planning. Make it a goal to do just a little bit, say, one block area every two weeks. You'll feel that you're making more progress that way, than if you are always comparing what you've done to the whole lot left to do. Remember when you were Planning, we said the only way to eat an elephant is one bite at a time! Every little stitch you make appears insignificant in itself, but added up makes a quilt. The little everyday acts you do add up to a lifetime, add up to success. Life is cumulative, and everything, every little stitch, counts!"

"Something else you can do is 'interrupt the pattern'," Grama advised. "Go out and do something totally different, you will come back refreshed. If you are bored with reading, go exercise. If you are bored with exercise, go read. The point is do something that uses different parts of your body and your brain.

"But the last and really important thing you have to do is: get out around people. I know it sounds weird but believe me, failure and giving up too soon often comes from isolation. When you wrestle with a dragon alone, it seems to get bigger all the time, to the point where you stop fighting. Go talk with people. Share your problems. Tell them what you are doing, and why, and you will hear your enthusiasm increase automatically as you re-capture your purpose. You may find they've faced similar dragons.

"Needless to say, you need to talk to positive,

supportive people who will re-energize you. And your enthusiasm, in turn, will energize them. Stay away from negative people who will steal your enthusiasm. You won't change them into positive people, but they will drag you down to their unhappy level. That's what 'misery loves company' means -- miserable people want you to join them in their misery. Avoid the moan-and-groan society who will give you tons of reasons why you'll fail. Don't listen to them. Remember, if your friends aren't successful and happy, don't take their advice.

"Which brings me to today's surprise," Grama re-directed the conversation. "I had a feeling by now you girls would be bored with quilting. This is usually the part where the glamour wears off because all the exciting planning and learning are over."

Grama continued, "It's all well and good to be positive and have proactive plans and intentions. That's relatively easy. It's also human nature at times to feel lousy and de-motivated. To deny these feelings is like we said about calling a problem, a challenge."

"I'll never make *that* mistake again!" Susan exclaimed.

"Therefore," Grama continued as if she wasn't interrupted, "it's essential to have fallback strategies, like the ones we discussed, to help yourself through those times. And so amazingly enough, the ninth Golden Thread is knowing how to cope with the unpleasant side of life!"

"If I didn't know better, Grama, I'd think you were just making these up as you go along," Jennifer exclaimed. "You seem to always know what is going to happen to us next!"

Susan hadn't listened to Jennifer's comment. She was still thinking about Grama's latest Golden

Thread. She brightened up then with a look of inspiration on her face.

"It sounds to me that the more self-confident you are, the better you are able to cope. And the more you know you are able to cope, the more self-confidence you have," she summarized the point of the lesson.

"That's excellent," I complimented her.

"See, we're getting better at this stuff. You could almost say there seems to be a 'thread' running through our lives now!" Jennifer joked, and Grama threw a pillow at her playfully.

"As I was saying! The Hamlet Quilt Guild is having a Quilt Show today and I bought tickets for us to attend. After that terrible pun it is obvious you need to air out your brains! Miss Stanton will be here at two o'clock with a wheelchair for me so we can zip around the show easier. In the meantime, girls, let's do lunch!"

I thought the wheelchair was an excellent idea. No point tiring old bones any more than necessary. Besides, Grama had slowed down a lot recently. Her enthusiasm for the girls and their quilts was as high as ever but she seemed to be moving slower and with deliberate concentration and effort. I know that if she was in pain she would not complain. She always denies the limitations of her age. Yet I noticed on her own quilt frame her progress had slowed to a crawl.

Perhaps she, too, was finally tired of the project. Having made so many quilts, how could she continue to be interested and find meaning? Silly question. Grama would always find meaning in her work because she would *give* meaning to the work. Perhaps she was just tired and I was worrying too much. The outing to the Quilt Show would probably do us all some good.

Over lunch I recounted to Jennifer and Susan my experiences of going to the quilt guild meetings years ago with Grama and her friends. I wasn't a member but it was fun to go along once in a while to observe how all the other women tackled their projects. It was a study in human psychology, and the patterns of behaviour that lead to success or failure.

Some women year after year went to every workshop and were continually starting a new 'block' pattern, starting some new project, yet never sewing all the blocks together, and never finishing anything. Other women sewed lots of quilt tops but didn't put them together into quilts. They would spend all the long hours sewing and correcting until they had a 'perfect' quilt top, then they would fold it away in a drawer, unquilted, unseen, unuseful, uncelebrated, while their enthusiasm carried them away on another project.

It was sad to see those women toil so hard, and deny themselves the satisfaction of completion before moving on. Quiltus interruptus, does not satisfy. At Show and Tell nights, they sat wistful and envious of the beautiful completed quilts on display, and promised themselves, yet again, to finish the next quilt, for sure.

There were women who would attend a workshop where the instructor carefully taught a new block pattern. They then hurried home to throw it all together in a race to be the first one back with a finished quilt. Sometimes it would have uneven corners, points that didn't meet, large uneven stitches, or any other sign of hasty careless work. Yet the

103

other ladies would all compassionately applaud her effort, and dutifully congratulate her on her speediness -- what else was there to praise -- while silently feeling a sad disapproval of poor workmanship. Sometimes a more experienced member would make gentle, helpful suggestions which more often than not went unheeded, if not unheard.

There were women who struggled mightily and who could make the simplest pattern into a major battleground of frustration and defeat. While one would give up, saying 'see, I can't do anything', her soul-sister would continue to fight every step of the way, struggling hard but always missing the ease of mastery. Both choosing to re-enforce 'life is a struggle' for themselves.

Of course the expert needlewomen were expert because '*they* were taught very young', or '*they* have no children, or spouse, or career to take their time', or '*they* were born with talent', or '*they* were just plain lucky'.

It amazed me how many reasons for success were ascribed to the experts, who took none on for themselves. The expert quilters were simply those women who continually learned about their craft, progressively challenged themselves and carefully applied themselves to both the grandness, and the drudgery, of the work. And, when it was all done, they stood in the limelight quietly, yet with satisfaction, savouring the moments of accomplishment before turning to guide and teach the younger women.

Jennifer and Susan had no pre-conception of what an impact the large community hall full of quilts would have on them. They were astonished by what

they saw in the Quilt Show. Dozens of quilts. Huge
queen size ones down to small wall-hanging size.
Every quilt was displayed fully flat, either hung on a
wall or suspended vertically from large frames, aisle
after aisle, like giant paintings in a gallery. And like an
immense museum of Art there were styles from
traditional to ultra modern. Moods from cheerful to
sombre, from elegant to whimsical. A rainbow of
emotions. And colours, tones and hues to shame a
rainbow. An exuberance of Life!

Grama happily guided the girls through the
show, pointing out design details and commenting on
levels of expertise. In one section we found the entries
in a 'challenge quilt' competition. Grama explained
that every quilter had been given identical sets of four
different fabrics. Their challenge was to make a quilt
that measured a certain size. The design was their
choice, and they could add up to two other fabrics.
The resulting twenty quilts, although containing the
same common ingredients, were totally unique and
different according to the added 'creativity' of the
quilters.

"This is *fascinating*, Grama!" Jennifer was
suddenly wide-eyed with revelation. "Every one of
these quilts is the same, yet every one is different.
Each one is a unique combination of the same
ingredients. And every one is beautiful! This is so
Right. It's just like you said a long time ago about
people -- value and celebrate the differences!"

As had happened to Susan with the zesty yellow
additions to her quilt, we could see Jennifer having
one of those 'Aha' reactions that was locking in a
lesson which until now was only a concept which
'sounded right' but had no real-ization. It seems the
strongest lessons we learn in life are the ones that

105

come to us as strong metaphors and with strong images. Jennifer now had a metaphor that would always remind her to see the differences in people as complementary and valuable. I hoped that tolerance and understanding would continue to mature into the wisdom I feel she is so capable of.

As we continued on we noticed there were several guild members in attendance, all wearing white gloves in order to handle the quilts with care and respect. Each 'guide' was happy to talk quilting with Jennifer and Susan. They shared their experiences -- many of the same problems the girls had been through. Hobbes wasn't the only cat ever to dismantle hours of work. And although many women said they truly enjoyed the quilting work itself, they nodded at Jennifer and Susan with true understanding, acknowledging the backbreaking tedium of it at times. Yet every woman said the lasting satisfaction they felt at completing the quilt far outweighed their discomfort.

Was this a message they needed to hear? You bet.

Occasionally one of the guild members would carefully turn back a quilt to reveal a different and sometimes elaborate pattern on the back. As we examined one particularly stunning quilt, Jennifer puzzled, "Why would anyone go to all the trouble of putting designs on the back, that no one will ever see?"

"Maybe to make it reversible?" Susan suggested.

"How about pride of workmanship?" I suggested.

"Edge," Grama commented quietly. The girls looked at her curiously so she elaborated. "Do you remember we talked about quality work? You can 'get by' in life by just meeting minimum standards of performance -- a work-to-rule mentality -- but quality work always exceeds customer expectations, even if it is simply to add a smile. It's called 'added value' and that's what gives you, or a company, an 'edge' on the competition.

"Is this a successful quilt? Is this the work of an expert needlewoman?" Grama asked.

"Sure," Susan replied, happy to display her new discriminating skill. "Look at the fine, even stitches, and detailed intricate design."

"Could the front of this quilt succeed by itself as a model of quality work?" Grama pursued.

"Sure," they nodded.

"The quilter didn't have to put anything else into it, did she? She chose to do so. She chose to 'exceed expectations', to go an extra mile for her customers, the user or viewer. That gave her an edge -- a *winning* edge -- an edge for success. Remember that. In a room full of accomplished and beautiful quilts, this one is truly outstanding!

"*This* is the result of Golden Thread #9: persevere through the tough times," she concluded.

We discovered that the woman who made the quilt was present and Jennifer and Susan were especially anxious to talk with her. They were effusive and sincere in their compliments and she just smiled sweetly, saying 'thank you' graciously. Their burning question was: how long did it take her to complete the masterpiece? How long had she struggled?

"People always want to know how long it takes to make a quilt. Every beginner wants to know what they're getting themselves into! The answer is: it varies. Like life. For some it's quick and easy, for others it's a long, long process. Depends on how much else you are doing, how focused you are. Myself, I work fulltime and have three teenage boys. This quilt took me nine years," she smiled anticipating their reaction.

"*Nine* years!" Jennifer whistled.

"Nine *years!*" Susan exclaimed.

All the way home in the car Jennifer and Susan relived their astonishment. Talk about changing their perspective. The Quilt Show had obviously been exactly what they needed.

Today had been a lesson re-enforced by a strong emotional experience. Grama's ninth Golden Thread -- coping with the tough times -- was a lesson they would not easily forget.

The girls had needed to 'get out around people', particularly a group of positive accomplished women who 'spoke' encouragement through their work and through the example they set.

Leave it to Yoda-Grama to know.

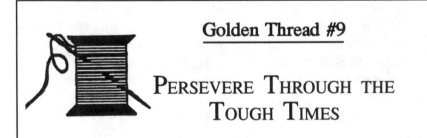

Golden Thread #9

PERSEVERE THROUGH THE TOUGH TIMES

July
"Pigs Can't Fly"

Jennifer and Susan were now slowly and steadily progressing through their quilting. Every once in a while I would hear someone yell "I'm p'd off!" and out she would go, to the movies, or to play tennis. A while later, she would be back quilting again.

Grama hasn't been feeling well lately, and she called a couple of times to postpone our monthly visit. Nothing to worry about she said -- she was "just feeling punky and not up to visiting". But let's face it, she's eighty-five and we worry.

As things turn out it was probably for the better. The girls were even busier with their summer activities. Susan's summer job is teaching crafts and games to schoolchildren. You might know, by the second week, one of their projects became a quilt to hang on the classroom wall. They used large brightly coloured scraps from their mothers' sewingbaskets and chunky, easy-to-handle yarn.

Here was Susan, who had not completed her own 'apprenticeship' with Grama, already starting to pass on her knowledge to her students. An ingenuous reminder that, in fact, we do not need to 'graduate' before we have something valuable to teach and give.

Naturally, she talked with them as they worked on the quilt, and out of that she had an idea to write a series of funny stories for children, teaching them Grama's Golden Threads in a simple child-appealing way. We've had lots of fun at the dinnertable kicking around ideas. The first story she wrote is called "Pigs Can't Fly" which is about a little girl on a farm and her pet pig. We think it's a real 'squeal'. Now she needs to find an illustrator, and a publisher, of course.

So far, Jennifer is happy with her job in Customer Service. The other day she came home with a new challenge -- she has to prepare a twenty minute presentation in her management training course. It's been a long time since made any speeches in high school, so she came to Susan and I, "her team", for help, and we brainstormed some ideas together.

"Of course, the essence of any presentation is communication so let's be clear about some of the basics of communication first," I suggested.

"You want to talk about talking?" Jennifer smiled. "I thought we already did too much of that!"

"Well, there is more to it than that, of course. But the important point is: even in a supposed one-way communication where you make a presentation to someone else, you have to understand your listener and speak accordingly. A presentation is never truly one-way, because you are responsible for the reactions you create in the other person. In other words, you are responsible for the response you receive from them.

"Therefore the first component of effective communication is understanding your audience. I've heard it described as 'seek first to *understand*, then seek to be *understood*'. In other words find out who your audience is first. What are *their* goals and interests? What do *they* need?"

"Like customer service," Jennifer realized.

"Exactly," I continued, "The second part of communication is presentation techniques that will improve the effectiveness of your communication. Susan, you can probably help Jennifer here with some ideas from your public speaking classes."

Susan nodded, "I think so. Remember, first of all you have to decide on an objective for your talk. What result do you want, for example -- to persuade, to motivate action, or simply to inform? Understanding the reason or motive for the presentation keeps you focused and helps you decide what content to put in or leave out."

"OK. That's good," Jennifer commented.

"Second. I'd suggest that you have to know what you are talking about. Do your homework, or research. Don't guess or try to fudge your way through. That calls for honesty and openness. I found out just how important that is in teaching children! Children are great at picking up on any unconscious signals you give that you are not being straight with them. Kids can be a deadly audience -- I guess, for me, that's what makes them a challenge to teach."

"Maybe I should give my speech to your class for practice!" Jennifer joked.

I added, "Susan is right. Knowledge and honesty build your credibility which means that your audience will be predisposed to listen to you, and believe you."

"That's all I can think of, Mom," Susan shrugged.

"That's OK. Those are two important points. Another consideration to add about the audience is: be courteous to the listener, or listeners, which you demonstrate several ways. Be concise and keep your presentation brief, that shows respect for their time, especially in a business setting.

"Be organized and logical in the sequence you present ideas. Don't make the audience have to work hard to understand you.

"Make sure you clarify what you say. Write it down if necessary and be sure everyone agrees on the content. Never assume everyone has the same meanings for the words you use. Clarity is the key to power in communication. It saves miscommunication and all the wasted time and emotion it causes.

"Also, the timing and pace of your presentation is crucial. Don't rush to fill silences. People listen a whole lot slower than you can talk. Leave them time to assimilate what you say otherwise your audience will drift off or become very irritated at you. Try to be creative and interesting in your presentation, use humour if you can, to keep the audience tuned in," I concluded.

"That's lot to remember all at once!" Jennifer exclaimed.

"True, it does seem to be a lot, but being a skillful, articulate communicator is essential to success in any career. The smartest person in the world is a failure if she cannot communicate her ideas understandably to others. So, like any skill, you need to practice, practice, practice, how you communicate with people. The more you do, the better you will get."

"Perfect practice makes perfect," Jennifer recalled Grama's words.

"Right."

"You can practice on us," Susan offered.

"Thanks, I will."

"Do these ideas help at all?" I asked. "Yes?

112

Good. Hopefully, Grama will be feeling better next month and I'm sure she, too, will have something to say about communication."

"You know, I'm beginning to suspect that you and Grama are in cahoots here, Mom." Jennifer drummed her fingers suspiciously on the table. "I'll know for sure if Golden Thread Number Ten turns out to be something about Communication!"

"Yeah, Mom. How much do you *really* know, Mom?" Susan also eyed me in playful suspicion.

"Ah, Madame Zelda knows all, sees all, and says nothing unless you cross her palm with silver!" I held out my palm but they shook their heads, no.

"I think we'll wait to get it straight from the source -- Yoda-Grama -- instead of the medium!" Jennifer laughed.

Golden Thread #10

COMMUNICATE EFFECTIVELY

August
"YOU STITCHED MY LIFE TOGETHER"

Lest you think otherwise, we hadn't forgotten about Robbie all this time. He, too, had a job and would be working out West all summer and unfortunately he wouldn't be home. However, we wrote and telephoned frequently.

After Jack died, Robbie spent a lot of time with Grama, 'just talking', you know, and since then he had kept up a regular correspondence with her. So, he was kept up to date on the quilting bee. If he thought we were all crackers he kept it to himself and whole-heartedly supported his sisters.

In fact, today we carried with us a package he sent to the four of us, addressed to: The Four Women of Ancient Wisdom, Holders of the Sacred Thimble, and Queen Bees of Success! Fortunately it was a large box and he had lots of room.

Naturally, we saved it to open with Grama and when opened we found four ceramic mugs, individually tagged, one for each of us. The card enclosed said: "Happy Unbirthday to all my favourite women. It's lucky you all have an Unbirthday on the same day. I found these in a craft shop and couldn't resist sending them. Love, Rob."

Each mug appropriately had a colourful quilt design on it and a caption.

Jennifer read hers first. It said: 'Quilting Forever, Housework Whenever!'

"He must have seen pictures of your room lately," I teased her. We all know she isn't the neatest person in the world, and of course all true 'feminists' hate housework. I keep telling her *everyone* hates housework.

Susan read her mug: 'The one who dies with the most fabric Wins!' Robbie had pegged her accurately -- she is a packrat, worse a sentimental packrat. She saves everything.

We all know, sewers are packrats, and quilters are the worst. However, as Grama likes to remind us -- a person who sews just *makes* scraps, quilters *use* them. Out of the rejected scraps, a quilter can make a work of art, using only her creativity and inner vision to 'add value' and give brand new meaning and purpose.

Back to the mugs. It's a good thing that the men who know us best also love us. Otherwise who knows what mine would say!

I laughed as I read mine: 'Quilters don't do Buttons!' That's an inside joke, I should explain. When Robbie was home for Christmas, although he did some not-too-subtle hinting, he never did get the buttons that were missing on two of his shirts sewn back on. I teased him at the time to 'get a girlfriend out West, or don't your New Age women do buttons!' He was having the last laugh.

Don't worry, he was taught to sew buttons on himself. He just didn't want to. Isn't that what mothers are for? Instead of putting young men in the army for a while to straighten them out, I think every young man should be given a job as a mother for a year. Tougher than any bootcamp. I'm kidding, of course.

Grama's mug had 'quilted' hearts on it and read: 'Thanks Grandma, You Stitched My Life Together.'

Grama went all soft at the sentiment. "What a nice kid," she sighed. Even frequent letters couldn't substitute for a real visit. She was obviously missing him, too.

"That's sweet," Susan hugged Grama as she read the mug. "Grama, that could be from any of us."

"You are so wise, Grama. You helped us all," Jennifer refrained. "How did you get to be so wise?"

"I just got old! Funny thing, you know, I said the same things forty years ago when I was your mother's age and nobody would listen," she twinkled. "Now I'm old everybody listens. Maybe people think I'll say something really brilliant before I die! Go figure," she shrugged.

"Thanks, Grama, maybe there's hope for me yet," I laughed.

"Since we received this 'communication' from Robbie let's talk today about communication for a while because it, too, is a Golden Thread, Number Ten."

"Aha! I knew it!" Jennifer exclaimed triumphantly.

"Yes, I understand from your mother, Jen, that you had to make a presentation at work, and that already gave you three an opportunity to discuss communication from a technical point of view. Have you talked about the 'message' that you are communicating?" Grama asked. The girls shook their heads.

"I thought we would leave that for you to cover,

Grama," I deferred.

"So, again you have a success 'how' but not a 'what'," she observed. "Well, you know, what you communicate is a lot more important than how you communicate it. For most people communication is just a lot of personality stuff -- a lot of flash and dazzle with no substance. That's because the message side of successful communication is much more difficult and time-consuming. It also requires careful thought. Yet it is also more satisfying because that is where you truly connect with people.

"However, first of all, before you can get a message across to anyone about anything you have to establish a meaningful dialogue -- meaningful to the other person. Building an effective dialogue requires three things: empathetic listening, an essence of caring and a willingness to share yourself with others.

"First, the empathetic listening means you focus your attention on the other person, in a non-judgemental way, to absorb not only the content of what they say, but also their feelings at the time. This can be tough because we naturally tend to filter what we hear through our own reality and re-interpret what someone says. Yet if you don't really understand and deal with the true emotions of other person -- which is their reality -- you don't truly communicate."

"Like Mom told us, seek first to understand, then seek to be understood," Susan volunteered.

"Right. Next, you must communicate that you care, and one of the ways you do this is by asking questions. Questions show that you are interested in the other person, interested to learn about them, that you value them. Questions may prompt people to reveal information or feelings that they would have been too shy to mention, or that they thought was

118

unimportant. And of course, you must listen to their answers, listen empathetically."

"Isn't that being nosey?" Jennifer asked.

"Some people think asking questions is invasive, or manipulative. I believe it isn't as long as you are sincerely interested, and more importantly, as long as you are also prepared to willingly share of yourself and make an honest response. There is a wonderful kind of power in sharing. Not a power of control, but a power of connecting to another human being. A true 'communion'."

I spoke up here, saying, "You certainly can't 'fake it, till you make it' where caring is concerned. If it isn't sincere, it isn't real and people will know. I once worked with a woman who was always asking questions, probing people. But it was as if she was simply studying a bug under a microscope. You didn't get the feeling that she cared at all about you, or was trying to understand you. She just wanted to use the information. You see, often the tip-off is whether you are also prepared to share something of yourself. People 'buy' ideas, or products, from people they feel an affinity for. Affinities form only when there is mutual caring, and sharing."

"So, asking questions isn't manipulative if you have the right intention behind it," said Jennifer. "OK. But what if you care and are open with someone else and they do use the information against you? Boy, I see that all the time around the office. You know, the old 'smile at your face and stab you in the back routine'."

"If you have given information about yourself freely and openly, how can it hurt you? People are usually afraid of their 'secrets' being found out. But if you willingly talk about yourself, no one can 'find you out'. The way I see it the only way to be truly invulnerable is to be vulnerable. In other words, to be open," Grama answered.

"The oak and the willow," Jennifer nodded.

"Right," Grama nodded.

"What's that?" Susan frowned.

Jennifer explained. "You know the story. Although the oak is strong and sturdy, in a strong wind it will break. It's strength is its downfall. On the other hand, the willow is soft and weak but in a strong wind it can bend and therefore survive because it is flexible. It's vulnerability actually makes it invulnerable. So openness is a vulnerability, but if it's my *choice*, it is an impenetrable defence."

"I get it," Susan nodded.

"To go back to the point," Grama redirected them. "Ask yourself this, do you want to play that office politics game the way others do?"

"No, but if I don't..." Jennifer trailed off.

"OK. So then, what's the worst thing that could happen to you? You get fired? Is that worse than losing yourself? Losing your self-respect? You can always find another job. Where can you find another you?

· "What we're really talking about here is Integrity which is exactly the 'message' we were leading up to. Living with integrity means knowing what your most important values in life are and consistently applying them throughout your life. This may be the hardest thing you do in life. That's why I make it the eleventh Golden Thread and not the first. I could have told you straight out months ago, as the first Golden Thread for Success, to have Integrity. Except that all the work you did building your character must come first.

"We started slow and easy for a reason. Do you remember the 'sampler' style quilts you've seen where each 'block' has a different pattern on it? Each block is designed to teach the new quilter a different, and increasingly difficult, lesson. When she has it finished, she has learned every quilting technique which she can then use to make any style quilt she chooses. In the same way, that's why we worked on each different 'block', or quality, of your character separately. Only now are you ready to stitch it all together.

"You developed who you are as a person by making those first choices about yourself. Who is it you want to be in life? What qualities do you admire in others and aspire to in yourself? Qualities like trustworthiness, self-discipline, confidence. What values do you intend to live by? Honesty, equality, respect may be some of those.

"Remember how each Golden Thread created a character trait? Making and keeping Commitments lead to Trust. Working through a Plan made you Self-disciplined. Quality Work gave you Self-esteem. Responsibility allowed you to have choices and therefore Independence. In order to Learn you had to stay flexible and to have Courage.

"Co-operation taught you how to work with people and be a team-player. Contribution balanced your selfish pursuits with a Selflessness. And knowing you were able to cope with the tough times built your Confidence.

"Then, as you began to live those qualities each day you started to see how those choices worked successfully for you. Life is a testing ground for your values. Once you know what kind of person you want to be, you make this additional, conscious choice to live with integrity.

121

"The choice itself seems easy. Everyone wants to live with integrity. But that can be harder than you expect because your integrity will be challenged many times, by people and situations.

"Your personal integrity, however, *is* that over-riding quality of character which demands that you hold to those values and consistently apply them in your life. It isn't easy. You may be forced to make tough, sometimes painful, decisions. And it can sometimes seem that the bad guy wins while the good guy loses. There are people who will try to sabotage you for being a person who does the Right thing. Either consciously or subconsciously they may envy your integrity or feel guilty because they haven't made the same Right choices for themselves.

"Business is just one example. Unfortunately, it also happens in personal relationships. But always remember, you can find another job, or another friend, or another lover. Where can you find another you?

"External loss may be the short-term cost of having integrity, but what is the alternative?" Grama asked. "As a wise man said: 'It profit not a man to lose his soul for all the world'."

Jennifer reflected this new insight back to us. "Now I understand what you were saying before about the price you may have to pay for success. If your choice is to have integrity, it could cost you in the office politics game, for example. But if integrity itself has a higher reward of being at peace with yourself -- it is worth it. Is that what it's all about, Grama? However you define success if it doesn't ultimately lead to peace of mind, it isn't success."

Grama nodded. "That is why the tenth Golden Thread is Communication and it leads directly into

122

the eleventh Golden Thread of Integrity. The most important message you can communicate to others is your values and your integrity.

"We've used your quilt throughout this past year as a metaphor for your life. I like to compare the eleventh Golden Thread, integrity, to the final and all important quilting stitches that hold the whole quilt together and give it definition as a unique thing. A quilt is a quilt is a quilt. It's not a layered blanket, and not a padded sheet. It is a quilt. No matter what outward 'personality' the surface pattern on the quilt exhibits, no matter how 'successful' or clever the block designs may be, it is the subtle quilting stitches that define its essence, its *quilt-ness*.

"You've seen how sometimes the quilting thread is almost invisible against the patterned fabrics. But if you hold it to the light, hold it up to examination, if you will, the quilting is revealed in the depth of texture and integrity it gives to the whole. The attention and uncompromising care given to the quilting is what validates the quilt.

"Likewise, in your life. You must know who you are and communicate who you are through your words and actions. Live with integrity as your highest ideal so that when your life is held up to examination you won't be found wanting."

In the car on the drive home there wasn't a lot of discussion about Grama's latest Golden Threads. Jennifer and Susan both seemed to be lost in thought.

As we neared home, Jennifer finally said, "Golden Threads Ten and Eleven -- Communication, Integrity. Wow, this is serious stuff, Mom. My brain is starting to hurt!"

I waited to reply.

123

"But it is all so important, Jen," Susan commented quietly.

"I know it is, but we still have one more Golden Thread to go. I can't imagine how tough that one's going to be! I'll bet Grama's kept a real doozie to the last!"

"I'm glad you girls are thinking seriously about all this. What Grama said this month is perhaps the most important message of all. That you have to live with integrity or you lose the best and most important part of who you are. And like Grama said, where can you find another you?

Golden Thread #11

LIVE WITH INTEGRITY

September
"Champagne Memories"

It was a quiet drive to Clareville today. Everyone was lost in her own thoughts. Grama has been very ill and the doctors tell us she may not be with us much longer. It seemed sudden, but at eighty-five not surprising. Perhaps we should have seen it coming. Would we have done anything differently?

The girls are upset. To be so young and to be reminded again that life doesn't go on forever, that cherished loved ones aren't immortal and won't be there forever, whenever we need their wisdom and comfort.

Susan had her arms clutched around her quilt bag just the way she held her teddy bear when she was a sad baby, unconsciously stroking the soft material.

"I wish we lived closer to Grama. We could have visited her more. We should have..." Jennifer pined.

I wish. We could have. We should have. Ah, Jen. Would we have? To live a life with no regrets.

I squeezed her hand, "It's OK, sweetie, Grama knows we all love her. Love is not always being right there with someone all the time. The love is there, even when you're not thinking of them. Grama is so proud of you guys. She gets a real big kick out of seeing her little birdies fly free. In the meantime, let's try to make it alright for her. OK? The greatest gift of love you can give her right now, is not to have her see you unhappy. OK?"

Two quiet sad faces looked at me. A quick exchanged glance at each other. Two faint but determined nods. And three deep breaths. OK, let's go.

Jennifer led the way. We can always count on her courage, to be noisy and funny and to cover her bad feelings with a smile.

"Hi, Yoda-Grama," she called out cheerfully, going over to the bed to give Grama a hug. "Look what we brought. Bet you thought we weren't ever going to finish!" as she pulled out her quilt. "Voila!" she unfurled her quilt gently over the bed.

"Today we celebrate," I hugged Grama. "The ordeal is over."

"Mine's done too, Grama," Susan squeezed in a hug and draped her quilt over a chair beside the bed where Grama could see.

"This is truly wonderful," Grama exclaimed softly as she examined the finished work. "I am so proud of you both. For a first effort, you have both made a beautiful top-quality quilt."

"And we owe it all to you, Grama," Jennifer said.

"*All*," I emphasized as I leaned over to kiss her. "And it *was* worth it."

"But not so fast," Grama interrupted, shaking her finger at us. "You have one more task to do. Remember, you have to date and sign your quilts. Here, I made signature labels for you and here is my waterproof marker. You write out your labels and sew them neatly to the back of your quilts. *Then* you are finished."

The girls were quick and eager to comply. As they nimbly slipstitched the labels on, I marvelled at how easily and nonchalantly they now worked. Their new dexterity gave maturity and confidence to their work.

Grama and I exchanged smiles. She nodded and continued, "This is the last and most important part. It's an important tradition to sign your quilt. In other words, take credit for your work. Always do work that you are proud to put your name on. That's an excellent discipline in itself -- knowing you will sign your name to your work is a good way to make sure you always do your best. And quality workmanship should always be honoured and celebrated!

"And so, the twelfth and last Golden Thread is Celebrate! Celebrate your accomplishments and feel proud of yourself. That will motivate you to keep doing things, the right things. You are both unique and valuable women and have so much to give. Stand up and take your place in the universe. Listen to your Yoda-Grama, she knows!

"Make sure the last thing you do is celebrate, your work, and your life. Life is too short not to be joyous and have fun.

"There, you finally have all the twelve Golden Threads. I hope they help you. So now, like Mr. Spock says 'Live long and prosper!'," she twinkled, raising a pontifical hand in the splayed-finger blessing. "And celebrate!"

"Right on, Grama!" Jennifer exclaimed.

"Boy, are we glad to hear that, Grama. We thought Number Twelve was going to be a real tough one, but this is one we can definitely handle!" Susan laughed and they both hugged Grama happily.

Twelve months had passed and twelve Golden

Threads for Success had been spun. Graduation day was here.

Lock in the good times, Jack used to say. So that is what we would do today. We would talk and reminisce on the year we had been through. We would laugh at the agonies and tease each other because that is the gentle way to laugh at someone else, with affection, while we laugh at ourselves, with forgiveness. We would applaud the breakthroughs and the growth. We would share our feelings, unguarded, because we were with women who listen, and care, and support.

Women do this so well.

We had brought glasses and 'champagne' -- a bottle of ginger ale to toast the victory of the completed quilts. Susan shook the bottle so it splattered and fizzed when opened. We all said 'pop' for the cork and sipped it quickly so it would tickle our noses and make us laugh. Silly, you say? Probably. Oh, well.

And we took pictures so we could remember and share the memories.

Grama tired quickly so we couldn't stay long. Soon there would be other longer, sadder, visits. I knew Grama wanted this special day to be all sunshine for Jennifer and Susan, to be a warm memory for them. So I started to make clean-up, wrap-up motions.

Grama looked at me, "Would you do me a favour, honey, and go tell Mrs. Wells I would like to see her for a few minutes after you leave today? Thank you."

This was a fairly transparent ploy to have me leave the room so I did as she asked. I guessed that there were some private words for the girls that

128

needed some space.

I was only gone a few minutes though, and when I returned Grama was holding the girls' hands while they fought back tears. Jennifer had a piece of paper in her other hand which she quickly folded and put in her pocket.

Grama patted their hands. "Now, now," she soothed. "Off you go. You have a long drive ahead. Give these old bones a hug before you leave. I am so *proud* of you both. Your beautiful quilts. And two beautiful talented young women. I know you are both going to do so well in life."

"We love you, Grama," they said as they hugged her again.

"I have one shot left," I said, lifting the camera. "Jen, Suz, with Grama, and the quilts," I directed and we 'popped' the flash on the last champagne memory.

The warm communion of the day, for a while left Jennifer and Susan peaceful and close to Grama, just as every visit does. Yet as we drove home in the bright sunshine, a sadness washed over them that they couldn't deny.

"What did you see today?" I asked.

"All of a sudden Grama seems so frail. She never used to seem so small and old," Jennifer remarked softly and sadly.

"A frail old lady we love who is slipping away from us," Susan added sadly.

"Frail in body, yes. But frail in spirit, never. Girls, I'm not going to tell you not to feel sad. But don't be sad for Grama. Don't regret not doing more. There is no unfinished business in your relationship with Grama. She knows you love her.

"That's what I saw today. A great deal of love.

129

And I am so proud of you both. You know, Grama is very pleased you let her teach you -- to make a quilt -- and, more importantly, all her Golden Threads for success. You gave her a great gift of love, by simply listening to her. You gave her the satisfaction, at the end of a long life, of knowing that she was able to pass on her knowledge and her wisdom to another generation. You let her complete her life. You let her fulfill a purpose. I'm very proud of you both.

"You know, at the beginning of your quilting odyssey we identified Grama as a role model -- for her expertise in quilting. And, as you quickly found out, she has lots to say about Life. Her words and her Golden Threads are only part of the lesson. Look at her life itself. There are subtle lessons there also. She may be telling you things by example that you are not even aware of."

"Like what, Mom?" Susan asked.

"Well, has Grama ever given you the feeling that she regrets anything in her life? No? Of course not. It isn't enough to say she has lived a good long life. She lived a *whole* life. Her life is an example.

"Grama has always been in harmony with herself and done what was right for her. And she has always done what she felt was ultimately Right. When that Congruency and Integrity meet you have true peace of mind. Grama has that. As you pointed out one time, that is the ultimate success, girls, to have peace of mind."

Jennifer and Susan nodded in thought-full silence and we drove the rest of the long way home in a lighter sadness.

Golden Thread #12:

CELEBRATE LIFE

October
"Fallen Leaves"

So now this is where I have to take over for Grama. Our beloved Yoda-Grama.

Grama died three days ago.

There are no words to describe the ache we all feel.

Forgive me that I can only leave the rest of this page blank with the sound of my heart beating in the emptiness.

November
"A PATTERN CHANGES"

The quilts are finished and without the regular trips to visit Grama we are all feeling lost. Not only for the special person we miss but also because a pattern in our lives has been changed forever, and the readjusting will take time.

Jennifer and Susan have realized that the sad happiness of Grama's death is that although her wisdom, humour and love was once only a telephone call away, now they have Grama's Golden Threads internalized as part of them, there is no distance at all between them. That has helped them to acceptance and peace of mind.

This is a time for healing. A time for remembrance and reflection.

135

December
"Everything With Love"

We made several trips to Clareville in the last three months. There were manydetails to wrap up, even for an old soul who lived simply. Today was a special, happier trip though. The Residence Director, Mrs. Wells, called last week and told us that Grama's friends wanted to give back to us all of her quilts she had made while she lived there. No ingratitude intended -- but as a gesture to give her love back, to us. A gift of love in the season of giving.

Jennifer and Susan were overwhelmed at the sight of over twenty quilts, cleaned and neatly folded on Mrs. Wells' desk. A tower of soft folds and a riot of colour kaleidoscoping into each other.

"Oh, Jen, they're so beautiful," whispered Susan as she picked up the top one gingerly and held it to her cheek in an automatic child reaction."

"This is wonderful," Jennifer replied brightly, taking the next one and letting the folds open freely, the quilt flowing from her arms.

"Can we go thank everyone?" Susan asked looking up at me.

"I think that would be a very gracious thing to do," I replied, taking the third quilt from the pile.

Guided by Mrs. Wells, we made our way slowly

from room to room, in some cases simultaneously saying first hello's and last goodbyes to the strangers who had all been Grama's friends. The Director introduced us as we went and told us bits of information about each resident. A blur of names and wrinkled faces and infirm hands. Many, many smiles.

On the way back to Mrs. Wells' office, as we passed through the lounge, she pointed out, "Here are Mrs. Shaw and Mr. Fulton," she introduced us as we approached two people seated in wheelchairs.

"Henry, these are Alice's girls, her grand-daughters Jennifer and Susan," she spoke louder with each word. "They've come to say Hello!"

"Bellow? I'm not bellowing, you are," he said grumpily.

"We want to thank you," I started but Susan interrupted.

"I remember you, Mr. Fulton. Your quilt is the extra soft one because you have trouble with your skin," Susan tried loudly.

"Thin? I've always been thin," he replied with a dismissing gesture. "Who'd you say you are?"

The girls laughed gently. "I'm *Jennifer*. This is *Susan*. We're granddaughters of Alice Myers."

"Alice? She's dead!" he yelled back. "Gone. Doesn't live here now. I already gave back the quilt she made me. Looked just like yours there," he pointed at me. "Gave it to her granddaughter. Well, you never know about girls. Mebbe she don't want it. If not she can give it back to me, then."

"Oh, Henry, just go on now," yelled Mrs. Shaw in the chair beside him. "He's deaf as a doorknob," she shook her head at the girls. "Never mind him," she continued and, taking Jennifer and Susan's hands firmly in hers, she looked at each of them intently and said, "Your Grama did everything with love." She shook their hands fiercely up and down as if to make the thought stick, that it was important to remember. "*Everything* with *love*," she repeated fiercely. She squeezed their hands and then let them go, waving them away.

Susan echoed softly to Jennifer as we continued down the hall. "Grama did everything with love."

Jennifer nodded. "Do everything with love. The last lesson, Suzie. If there are Golden Threads, there must be a Golden Needle. 'Do Everything With Love' is the Golden Needle Grama used to stitch all her Golden Threads through life," she said, putting her arm gently around Susan's shoulder.

"She had so much more to tell us," Susan pined sadly.

"No. I think she said it all. It all comes down to love. 'Do everything with love'," Jennifer reassured Susan.

I nodded to myself as I followed behind them. Grama could still speak loudly to the girls. We are immortal as long as we live on in people's memories.

Back home, we hurried to unpack the car so we could explore our treasures one by one.

"Look, Mom," Susan drew my attention to something we hadn't noticed before. "There's a note pinned to this quilt."

"What does it say?" I asked putting down another bundle.

"It's a list. There's names and dates," she looked puzzled.

"Here's another one, on this quilt," said Jennifer holding up a corner with one hand, flipping through the rest of the pile with her other. They looked at each other. Every quilt had a note pinned carefully to the back of one corner.

"These are all the people who had the quilt," said Jennifer, suddenly inspired. "Look. 'Mr. King, died February 18, 1987', then 'Mr. Charbonneau, died June 27, 1989', then 'Mrs Epstein', no date," she read.

"Because she's still alive," Susan jumped in. "We met her. She was wearing that funny fox collar, remember. She must have had this quilt last. We know that Grama gave the quilts away and if that person died Grama would have the quilt washed and give it to someone else."

"This is weird," said Jennifer. "Look at this," she said finding another note, "This one goes back twenty years. It must have been one of the first quilts Grama made at the home. Look at all the names."

"Now, don't unpin them," I warned. "Let's not get the notes all mixed up."

"This is amazing. All these people. Wow!" Susan enthused, picking up one after another and finding the note on each. "All these people," she repeated in amazement.

From a small personal quilting hobby and a love of people, Grama had unwittingly touched many, many lives over the years. Like drops in a bucket, each small act of love had added up to more than a full measure.

"Who did all this?" Jennifer wondered aloud.

"I think probably the Director, Mrs. Wells," I offered. "It was very kind of her to go to all this effort for us," I joined the girls in their amazement and pleasure.

"It must have been quite a job to track down the history of each quilt," Susan observed. "We should write to her and thank her," she suggested and we nodded agreement.

Over the days that followed, we wallowed in quilts. It was a joy to examine each one. To see the colours, sometimes bright and gaudy, other times somber and moody. We wondered aloud at what Grama had been thinking at the time, what kind of mood she had been in while working on each quilt.

Sometimes the stitching was smooth, even and confident. Sometimes it was a little shaky. Had she been ill at those times in her life? Or just tired and inattentive. She told us once that a quilt is a self-portrait of the person who made it. If that is true, then a quilt can also be a biography of the quilter, if we are perceptive enough to read the subtle clues. There could be no better biography of Grama's life than the body of work she left behind.

Searching through her books and magazines we found the traditional names for the quilt designs and laughed at the funny-sounding names like 'Turkey Tracks', 'Monkey Wrench' and 'Kitten in the Corner'. Names from the pioneer women who were *her* grandmothers. We discovered their names, and naming them, they became ours.

We were sad when we realized the sombre navy, grey and white quilt called 'Storm at Sea' was made the year after Jack died. We re-named it Daddy's Quilt and the girls put it on my bed.

Jennifer and Susan decided to catalogue the quilts so I bought them a photo album. We photographed each quilt, labelled the photo and placed it in the book next to the note that had been pinned to it.

Freed from the concern of damaging or

confusing the identifying notes, now we could really
enjoy Grama's quilts. We piled them on our beds,
draped them on chairs and hung each in rotation on
the wall over the livingroom sofa.

One evening, after we had more or less returned
to our normal routines, Jennifer said pensively, "You
know, Mom, we really should do something with
Grama's quilts."

"Like what?" I asked.

"I don't know," she hesitated. "I feel sort of bad
that we have them all here. Grama made them for
other people to enjoy. You know, at the home.
People who needed them."

"You don't want to give them back, do you?"
Susan asked in alarm, putting down the book she was
reading.

"Well no, of course not. I mean I feel like I
should give them back but I don't *want* to. I feel so
selfish. Does that make any sense?" she asked me.

"Of course it does," I assured her. "Is there any
other way that you could still keep the quilts but that
other people could enjoy them, too?"

"Loan them out to old folks, I guess," she
shrugged weakly.

"What about putting them in a Quilt Show?"
Susan suggested.

"Do you think a show would take Grama's
quilts, Mom?" Susan asked.

"Wait a minute. Why don't we make our *own*
show. We could do that, couldn't we, Mom?" Jennifer
declared.

"Sure," I started to say, "but..."

"You bet we can, Jen," said Susan emphatically.
"Grama taught us everything we need to know to be
successful at anything! Remember, the Golden

Threads!"

"Right on! What's the first Golden Thread? Make a Commitment," Jennifer answered her own question.

"OK. I will if you will, pardner," Susan put out her hand for Jennifer to shake. "How about you, Mom?"

"Glad you remembered I'm here," I kidded.

"Sorry, Mom. But Suz, I think if we do this, we should do it ourselves, right? You understand, Mom, don't you?" Jennifer asked.

"Of course I do. But can I listen in?" I replied.

"Sure," she nodded. "So, Jen, now we're committed. Or should be!" Susan laughed.

"Next, we visualize the outcome: by seeing in our mind's eye, all Grama's quilts on display and lots of people coming to admire them. Then, we find a role model, an expert, and do what they do," Jennifer recalled.

"The women who organized that quilt show we saw last summer might advise us, or be able to suggest someone who can," Susan suggested. "That's what you called mentoring, isn't it, Mom?" I nodded yes.

"Good idea. Now, Golden Thread Number Two: set a goal. That would mean we describe exactly what we want to do and set a date for it," Jennifer recalled. "Then Golden Thread Number Three: we need a Plan. We have to write it down, and remember all the S-T-E-P-S," Jennifer continued. "Keep it Simple. Have a Time-frame for each action item to be finished by. Keep it Efficient by balancing time against accuracy."

"We have to Prioritize the Plan, by what's most important first, and how urgent it is. Do first things first," Susan finished. "And Start now, don't forget," she added.

"Next. We have to take Responsibility -- Golden Thread Number Four -- and be flexible if something goes wrong," Jennifer was nodding her head 'yes' remembering 'the Hobbes incident' and herself, and smiling.

"Golden Thread Number Five: always do Quality Work. Let's face it, this will be the best quilt show ever!" exclaimed Susan confidently. She continued, "And Grama's Golden Thread Number Six: learn from our mistakes as we make them, and keep going on. I almost forgot our 'post-graduate lesson'. We have to 'add zest' by stretching ourselves, but since we've never made a quilt show happen before, this whole thing is definitely out of our comfort zones!" She was remembering her own former lack of confidence.

"What else?" Jennifer was thinking. "We covered all the 'inner work' -- Commitment, Goals, Planning, Responsibility, Quality Work and Learning."

"What about Co-operation?" I suggested.

"Hey Mom, come on now. We're sisters. When do we ever *not* co-operate?" Jennifer hugged Susan and they laughed.

"Of course. Silly me," I mocked back.

"Mom's right. Golden Thread Number Seven: Co-operation. This really is a win-win situation," Susan observed. "We get to keep the quilts *and* other people get to enjoy them too."

"Maybe we could charge admission and give the money to charity, or to the old folks home at Clareville," Jennifer suggested as her enthusiasm gathered speed, and their ideas continued to tumble out.

"What a great idea! Grama would like that. Contribute to society, make a difference in people's lives. Golden Thread Number Eight," Susan supported the idea.

"If we become discouraged or de-motivated, or catch the p-moan-ia bug, we know how to cope: by taking Grama's p-medicine of patience, perfection, perseverance, persistence and pride," Jennifer recalled Golden Thread Number Nine. "We also remember to 'get out around positive people' – like other quilters!"

Susan again picked up the theme. "Grama's Golden Threads Number Ten and Eleven. Communicate Integrity is the biggest challenge of all and the most important. Fortunately, the next one, Number Twelve: Celebration, is the easiest. We can certainly make our Quilt Show a joyful celebration!"

"You bet!" Jennifer nodded and put out her hand this time, and they shook hands to seal the agreement. "Let's do it!"

"And let's not forget, 'Do everything with Love'," Jennifer reminded them, and Susan nodded. They were quiet for a moment as a sad stormcloud passed between them, then quickly brightened again as it drifted away.

"What will we call the show, Jen?" she asked.

"I don't know. Let's see. How about 'A Celebration of Quilts'?" she offered. "Or 'A Life in Quilts'?"

"Nah, it's been done before. I saw it in one of Grama's magazines," Susan countered.

"How about 'Grama's Quilts: Yesterday and Today'?"

"Um. 'Quilts: A Way of Life'?"

"I've got it, 'Grama's Quilts: A Way of Life'!"

"No. It should be 'Grandmother's quilts'."

145

"Right. And 'A *Woman's* Way of Life'."
"That's it!" they chorused, 'Grandmother's Quilts: A Woman's Way of Life'!"

Spring
"FULL CIRCLE"

It's April again. Spring is breaking out everywhere. Robbie will be home soon. He made excellent marks at university. This summer he decided he wants to work closer to home, in order to catch up on some homecooking!

Jennifer was promoted last week to Assistant Customer Service Manager. She is talking about moving into her own apartment. I've been hearing a lot about one particular fellow named Jim so I guess it's time we had him over for a family dinner, inspection, and close order drill!

Susan did extremely well at Teacher's College. In her practice teaching weeks, one school principal was so impressed with her maturity and confidence, he suggested she apply for a summer school job with them, and indicated he would consider her for a fulltime job when she graduates.

So I'm a happy and proud Momma.

Yes, the Quilt Show opened last Saturday.

The girls enlisted the local Quilt Guild to help. There they found many talented, experienced women and made new friends. The guild members were so intrigued with the idea and so impressed with Jennifer and Susan many volunteered their time and lots of helpful advice for organizing their Show.

Funny how word travels. That network of women who talk, and share, and care. That connectedness many men haven't come to understand and too often dismiss.

When news spread of the show dedicated to the life of Alice Myers and her quilts, strangers from all over started to write to us. Grama's old friends, with memories. Young relatives of the people in the home, with thanks. All their contributions were added to the show. A dozen more quilts arrived, to be displayed, and then to be kept by the girls.

We reach out to touch and we never know how the touch will be returned.

One of Grama's quilts came just last week. Old and worn and faded and much used, as a well-loved quilt should be. It was barely recognizable. The note said, "I'm sorry this quilt is in such bad shape. I've washed it many times. My aunt gave it to me I can't remember how many years ago. She told me stories about your grandmother and living on the farm. She always said Alice was the kindest person she ever knew."

Not a bad way to be remembered, I thought. The kindest person she ever knew: a suitable legacy for a successful life. Grama would have been pleased, I'm sure.

I hope to be so fortunately labelled after I'm gone.

Early Saturday morning before their Quilt Show opened Jennifer and Susan took me on a VIP tour, my first glimpse of the culmination of all their efforts.

At the front of the hall, the girls had an enlargement of the last photo of Grama, with them,

and their quilts. Beside it they wrote the story of how
Grama, their Yoda-Grama, taught them her Twelve
Golden Threads -- how to live and build their
character and to be successful in life. They added their
own insight: that the Golden Needle, 'Do Everything
With Love', stitched it all together.

Jennifer and Susan had taken Grama's last,
unfinished, quilt and secretly finished the quilting and
binding. "It's a surprise. You'll see it in the Show,"
they told me when I pried. The sewingroom had been
"action central"and off-limits to me for months. And
there at the front door was Grama's last quilt. 'Hearts
and Roses'. So distinctively Grama. There were the
hearts cut from Jack's old shirt. There were even
some scraps from Jennifer and Susan's quilts worked
into the pattern, along with dozens of other fabrics, all
scraps from a lifetime, all favourite memories.
Whoever said "God gave us memory so we would
have roses in December", must have known Grama.

"Look, Jen," I pointed, "There's the material
from the sunsuit Grama made when you were three.
You were wearing it in the photos taken the summer
we spent at Graham Lake. I remember you making
mudpies -- for the bar-b-q! And Susan, there's material
from your first fancy dress for the teen dance. Ever
wonder what happened to that boy, Roger, you went
with?" Susan shrugged and smiled at her own
memories.

You might know Grama would weave all those
memories into her last quilt. As if this way she could
continue to talk with us and reminisce. Grama would
always be part of Jennifer and Susan. And Robbie.
And I.

We live on in the people and the legacy we leave
behind.

149

"Oh, girls, this is so beautiful," I exclaimed as we stood with my arms around their waists, admiring her masterpiece. I hugged them as I looked over the detailed applique and fine quilting stitches -- Grama's, Jennifer's and Susan's, all intertwined. Threads connecting the generations.

"It's for you, Mom," Jennifer squeezed me back.

"Grama wanted *you* to have this quilt," Susan confirmed.

"She was making it for you," Jennifer nodded.

"How do you *know* that?" I queried with tears starting.

"She told us, Mom," Jennifer gently explained. "When we saw her in September. Remember when she asked you to talk to Mrs. Wells?"

"That was just to make you leave the room," Susan expanded.

"She told us when you left. Read the signature plate on the back, Mom. Grama had written out what she wanted us to put on it for her," Jennifer went on. "She knew she wasn't going to be able to finish it and that made her sad but we promised we would carry on for her."

Yes, these girls would carry on for Grama. They would continue to learn and grow. They would use their experiences to become wise; and in their turn they would hand on the tradition, and their wisdom, to other young women. Life would come full circle and continue.

"We embroidered it on. By hand, of course," Susan said proudly.

"We used some shiny gold thread we found in a craft shop," Jennifer pointed out. "We thought Grama would like that."

I turned back the bottom right hand corner and

there was the neatly lettered dedication in Golden Thread:

> *To Angela*
> *Given with Love unending*
> *For Love given unmeasured*
>
> *Alice Myers, 1905-1990*
> *Completed by her granddaughters*
> *Jennifer and Susan Patten*
> *March 31, 1991*

Grama's Golden Threads

MAKE A COMMITMENT

SET A GOAL

PLAN YOUR WORK & WORK YOUR PLAN

ALWAYS DO QUALITY WORK

TAKE RESPONSIBILITY & BE RESPONSE-ABLE

MAKE LIFE-LONG LEARNING A HABIT

CO-OPERATE

CONTRIBUTE & MAKE A DIFFERENCE

PERSEVERE THROUGH THE TOUGH TIMES

COMMUNICATE EFFECTIVELY

LIVE WITH INTEGRITY

CELEBRATE LIFE

Grama's Golden Needle

Do Everything
With Love

A Note from the Author

During the twenty years I've been in business and consulting I've read dozens of "success" books and attended countless self-improvement seminars and I have found the following recurrent problems. First, your success is often equated with money, power and fame, with the appeal to our basic fears and greed. Second, the programs too often are a quick-fix solution based on "personality" tricks, rather than the development of character based on values. And third, an externally driven time-management system replaces an internally driven self-management.

I believe there is a softer, gentler message to be told. One of values and integrity and one that is closer to life, reality and work as most women know them.

Many "how-to" or "success" programs are developed by, and are about, men, using male business, sports or warfare models and metaphors. The sometimes gratuitous, and sometimes genuine, dissembler being a "by the way, if you are a women, this applies to you also". I did not set out to write a stridently woman's book. I like men, a lot. But I did want to write a book that uses a strong woman's metaphor. Thus from my own many hours spent quilting, and thinking, and creating, came this book.

I hope someday we come up with a different word for "mentoring" that will reflect the way women support and nurture others – in terms of their emotional needs, rather than just factual how-to-do-the-job terms. Let me know if you hear of one.

In fact, I would be pleased to hear from you anyway. I wish you all the best and peace of mind.

Aliske Webb
Toronto 1992

157

Twelve Golden Threads

If you enjoyed this book...

It makes a wonderful gift
for Mother's Day, Christmas
Valentine's Day, Birthdays...

Use the Order Form below and forward to:
The Quilt Inn Printworks Inc.
24 Farmcrest Drive
Scarborough, Ontario
Canada M1T 1B7

Phone (416) 490-8278

Please forward _____ copies of Twelve Golden Threads to me
or someone I love: (We will enclose a gift card from you)

Name: _____

Address: _____

_____Postal/Zip_____

Method of Payment: ☐ Cheque enclosed

☐ Visa   ☐ American Express

Card # _____ Expiry Date _____

Signature _____

Amount: _____ x $ 9.95 = $ _____

Postage & Handling $ 3.50
(Ont. residents add 8% PST)
(Cdn. residents add 7% GST) $ _____

TOTAL $ _____